PHILOSOPHY AND
CYBERNETICS

PHILOSOPHY AND CYBERNETICS

Essays Delivered to the
Philosophic Institute for Artificial Intelligence
at the University of Notre Dame

*Frederick J. Crosson and
Kenneth M. Sayre,
Editors*

UNIVERSITY OF NOTRE DAME PRESS
Notre Dame   London

Copyright © 1967
UNIVERSITY OF NOTRE DAME PRESS
Notre Dame, Indiana

Library of Congress Catalog Number: 67-16858
Manufactured in the United States of America

TO OUR MOTHERS

Preface

THE PHILOSOPHIC INSTITUTE FOR ARTIFICIAL Intelligence was established in 1965 by the University of Notre Dame. Its charge was to study, constructively and without polemic, the interaction between computer technology and various philosophic conceptions of the nature of man. In accord with this purpose, sponsorship was established under the Department of Philosophy, the Computing Center, and the Center for the Study of Man in Contemporary Society.

Undoubtedly the most significant technological development during the mid-century has been the construction of general purpose computers capable of performance which in man would be deemed intelligent behavior. Inasmuch as these machines, however complicated, are artefacts, this capability has come to be known as "artificial intelligence." The term 'artificial,' however, should not be taken in any sense to indicate inferiority. In its performance of mathematical calculations and in the control of complex systems the computer generally is recognized as superior to the human being, and there are many workers in the field of artificial intelligence who seriously believe that there are few, if any, intellectual tasks which will not some day be fully within the competency of a skillfully programmed digital computer.

Among philosophers informed in such matters there is now a fairly general agreement that the possibility of artificially intelligent mechanisms will force some basic changes in our conception of intelligent behavior in the human being. The editors share this agreement but are convinced that a responsible commentary on the issues of human and mechanical intelligence is possible only against the background of a thorough familiarity with both the philosophic and the technological problems involved. Philosophic discussions of artificial intelligence, increasingly numerous during recent years, too often reflect less than a close acquaintance with computers and tend thereby to be overly speculative and technically unrealistic. When left to philosophically untutored computer specialists, on the other hand, commentary on such matters seems to involve more gross misconceptions about human mental behavior than can be overlooked in the name of charity from a responsible philosophic point of view. In hopes of striking a fruitful balance between these two extremes, the Institute was staffed with specialists in several fields, including (among the scientific) information theory, computing science, and biology, and (among the philosophic) phenomenology, theory of perception, and philosophy of mind. Each member, moreover, shared considerable interest in the others' technical problems, and all had in common a lively interest in understanding the import of computer technology for the sciences of man.

Apart from the goal of competent commentary on matters of artificial intelligence, it is our conviction further that the use of computer models will prove valuable as a technique of philosophic criticism and analysis. A sign of the thoroughness with which the operations of mathematical calculation are understood is the considerable skill which has been demonstrated in programming computers to perform these operations without subsequent human intervention. One of the main reasons we are not able to program the creative skill of the poet or composer into the computer, on the other hand, is that we do not understand these skills as well as those of the mathematical reckoner. In the attempt to achieve rudimentary creative skills with a computer, however, we will become able to identify more precisely those aspects of the creative process of which our understanding is most inadequate, and will be able consequently to improve our understanding through analytic attention more carefully directed upon these puzzling features. The mark of a mature understanding of aesthetic creation, then, would be either the ability to duplicate such behavior through a properly programmed computer or the ability to specify exactly (and without philosophic partisanship) why such behavior cannot be simulated in this fashion. This approach, we believe, shows particular promise as well for the analysis of pattern recognition, decision making, and memory, capacities in which the computer already possesses a moderate degree of talent.

Not all the possible benefits of this approach are in favor of the philosopher exclusively. The path of interaction between philosophic analysis and computer simulation permits passage in both directions, and it seems inevitable that a more precise and articulate conception of what is involved in the intelligent behavior of human beings will result in an increased ability to program this behavior into a sufficiently capacious digital computer. What is not understood cannot be simulated. Conversely, what is well understood is far more likely to be successfully simulated than some puzzling aspect of behavior which only chance or blind inspiration could transfer into a computer program. Just as the attempt to program a basic mental skill into a computer can result in an increased understanding of the skill itself, so an increased conceptual grasp of a skill will aid considerably in bringing that skill within the competency of a computer-based mechanical system. With this in mind, members of the Institute are actively engaged in computer simulation, efforts thus far being concentrated upon the achievement of a flexible handwritten character recognition program.

During the academic year 1965–1966 the Institute sponsored a series of seminars bearing upon the philosophic implications of recent developments in cybernetics and information theory. Seminar leaders were invited to discuss issues close to their own professional interests but asked at the same time to direct their remarks to a general university audience. This accounts for the fact that the papers in this volume, although dealing with problems currently on the frontiers of their respective areas, contain a considerable amount of introductory material. The dual purpose of reaching both specialists and interested laymen in these several areas was emphasized again when the participants were asked to expand their papers in view of joint publication. Insofar as these aims have been reached, the essays in the present volume provide material of interest not only to specialists in problems of artificial intelligence but to the general college reader as well.

The same circumstances of origin account for the minimal overlap among several essays in their presentation of the basic formulations of information theory. Rather than collect this material into a single essay on the subject, we considered it advantageous to allow each essay to develop just the formulations needed for its particular purpose. At the expense of a small amount of repetition, we have thereby preserved the autonomy of each essay and made it possible for a reader to select essays of particular interest to him without reading others as a necessary preparation.

With these considerations in mind, we hope that the present volume will be suitable for supplementary reading in college and graduate courses in philosophy of mind, philosophy of man, and artificial intelligence. We hope also that it will prove useful to a more diversified college audience concerned for various reasons with the impact of "intelligent machines" upon traditional notions of the uniqueness of the human being.

Contributors to this volume all teach at the University of Notre Dame. They are Professor James Massey of the Department of Electrical Engineering, currently Visiting Associate Professor of Electrical Engineering at the Massachusetts Institute of Technology; Associate Professor Frederick Crosson, Director of the General Program of Liberal Studies; Associate Professor Kenneth Sayre of the Department of Philosophy, Director of the Philosophic Institute for Artificial Intelligence and currently Visiting Fellow at Princeton University; and Assistant Professor David Burrell, C.S.C., of the Department of Philosophy.

Grateful acknowledgement is due the National Science Foundation for its support of much of the research from which these essays originated. Among persons we wish particularly to thank are Dr. George Shuster, Dr. Donald Mittleman, and The Reverend Ernan McMullin for their encouragement and in many forms their support. We wish finally to acknowledge the versatile assistance of Mrs. Norma Davitt, patient artist of the typescript, and to thank our wives for their constant support and cheerful understanding.

FREDERICK J. CROSSON
KENNETH M. SAYRE

Contents

Preface vii

I. INTRODUCTION

1. Philosophy and Cybernetics 3
   K. M. Sayre

II. INFORMATION THEORY

2. Information, Machines, and Men 37
   J. L. Massey

3. Choice, Decision, and the Origin of Information 71
   K. M. Sayre

4. Information Theory and Phenomenology 99
   F. J. Crosson

5. Toward a Quantitative Model of Pattern Formation 137
   K. M. Sayre

III. ON CERTAIN CAPACITIES IN MEN AND MACHINES

6. Memory, Models, and Meaning 183
   F. J. Crosson

7. Obeying Rules and Following Instructions   203
   D. B. Burrell

8. Instrumentation and Mechanical Agency   233
   K. M. Sayre

   Selected Bibliography   263

I. Introduction

PHILOSOPHY AND CYBERNETICS

K. M. Sayre

INTRODUCTION

THERE IS NO RECOGNIZED PHILOSOPHIC THEORY or school which could properly be termed 'cybernetic,'[1] and philosophers outside the Soviet Union have been slow even to acknowledge problems of cybernetic origin. Within the past few years, however, philosophic publications inspired by developments in information theory and in the theory of computing machinery have begun to appear in increasingly substantial numbers, and the "mind-machine" problem at least is presently recognized as a standard issue of philosophic debate.

It is appropriate, therefore, to undertake a review of the current impact of cybernetics upon philosophy with (1) a survey of philosophic issues stemming from information theory and (2) a discussion of the mind-machine problem from the point of view of computing science. This review is terminated with (3) an estimation of the relevance of these topics for the traditional problems of mechanism, physicalism and determinism.

INFORMATION AS A TECHNICAL MEASURE

Use of the term 'information' in its current technical sense can be traced back to the attempt by Hartley to construct a quantitative measure of the relative transmission capacities of electrical communication systems.[2] Hartley's measure was a logarithmic expression in terms of the binary decisions necessary to characterize a given message state uniquely, and the quantity measured by this expression was called "information." This usage was continued by Shannon, Wiener, and Brillouin, who differed, however, in their designations of the science in which informational characteristics of communication systems are studied. Shannon spoke of the mathematical theory of communication;[3] Wiener coined the term 'cybernetics;'[4] and Brillouin chose the title 'information theory.'[5] Choice between 'communication theory' and 'information theory' remains largely a matter of taste, although the latter will be used exclusively in this discussion.

Information is a statistical function of alterations within a communication system including: (1) a sender capable of selecting a specific set of message states out of a range of possible states; (2)

a channel through which the selection of the sender can be indicated; and (3) a receiver capable of decoding this indication to determine the specific message states selected by the sender. Before the selection of any particular message state there is an a priori probability less than 100 per cent that it will be the state selected, of which the receiver is assumed to be in some sense informed. After selection of a particular state, the probability of selecting that state changes to 100 per cent, and the indication of this change in probability to the receiver is the transmission of information through the communication system. Thus information in the technical sense is a change in probabilities indicated to the receiver as the result of actual selection among possible message states by the sender at the opposite end of the communication channel.

The amount of information conveyed from sender to receiver is a direct function of the change in probabilities indicated to the receiver. In a simple communication system in which the sender is capable of selecting among only two possible message states (for example, yes and no) of equal probability, indication of either state to the receiver will change the probability of that state from 50 to 100 per cent. In this instance the probability of either state is doubled by its indication to the receiver, and one bit of information is conveyed by each message through the communication channel. If the probabilities of selecting yes and no are 25 and 75 per cent, respectively, however, indication of yes to the receiver will double its probability two times over and thereby convey two bits of information, whereas indication of no will increase its probability by a factor only of 0.4, thereby conveying 0.4 bits of information. Since more uncertainty is removed by a change from 25 to 100 per cent than by a change from 75 to 100 per cent, more information is conveyed by the former than by the latter change. In general, the amount of information in bits (binary digits required to indicate the selection) conveyed by the correct transmission and reception of a given message state is equal to the number of times the initial probability of that state must be doubled to reach 100 per cent.[6]

In actual communication channels indication of message states is seldom uniformly accurate, and transmission typically is in terms of ensembles rather than single message states. The amount of information conveyed to the receiver varies both with the reliability of the channel and with the nature of the ensemble, and one of the major contributions of information theory is to provide equations by which specific channels can be matched with specific message ensembles with maximum efficiency. In general the less information conveyed with a given message ensemble, the greater its redundancy and the greater the likelihood accordingly that it will be transmitted accurately through an unreliable or noisy communication channel.

INFORMATION AND MEANING

The concept of information in the technical sense provides a purely quantitative measure of communication transactions which abstracts entirely from the interests and meanings of the agents involved. Within information theory it is indifferent even whether the sender and receiver are capable of using language with semantic meaning. Yet there has been a tendency from the beginning, despite Hartley's[7] and Shannon's[8] cautions to the contrary, to confuse this technical sense of information with the semantic content of sentences in a natural language. In an early paper on the problem of Maxwell's "demon," Szilard suggested that the selective activity of the demon is based on information about the motions of the gas molecules which he accordingly alters, and hence that the demon changes information into diminished entropy.[9] Information of the first sort is akin to semantic information, whereas entropy in thermodynamics is formally the same as the lack of information in the technical sense of information theory. Wiener later made Szilard's implication explicit by asserting that information may be interpreted as the negative of the entropy of a message. "That is, the more probable the message, the less information it gives. Clichés, for example, are less illuminating than great poems."[10] Contrary to this interpretation it has been argued effectively on several occasions[11] that information in the technical sense is entirely distinct from whatever meaning may be conveyed by the message states which information theory studies, and most technical writers have joined in this opinion.

But philosophers and others interested in semantics have often expressed hope that information theory would provide clues for a deeper and more precise understanding of the semantic aspects of human communication. Weaver, although acknowledging the disparity between technical and semantic information as such, has announced his conviction that because of information theory we are ready now for a "real theory of meaning."[12] And Bar-Hillel, after denying any relevance of the technical concept of information to semantics, suggests that the calculus which information theory employs might itself turn out to be a powerful formal tool for semantics and semiotics.[13] However, to date no comprehensive extension of the formalism of information theory has been accomplished. For present purposes it is best merely to review certain similarities and differences between technical and semantic information upon which any eventual alliance between information theory and semantics will have to be based.

ENTROPY OF NATURAL LANGUAGE

Despite the disparity between technical information and meaning, any communication in a natural language can be assigned a measure in bits of information. This measure in any particular instance is a function of the probabilities of occurrence in the language of the several symbol combinations within the communication. The less frequent the symbol combination (versus propositional-expression) within the language in question, the more information (versus meaning) is conveyed by its occurrence. Since vowels generally occur more frequently than consonants, less technical information is conveyed by words with a high proportion of vowels than by words of comparable length with a high proportion of consonants. Similarly, less information is conveyed by the single occurrence of letter E than by the occurrence of any other letter in most languages using that symbol.

Given frequencies of occurrence of all letters within a given language, the information theorist can calculate the average information content of any message formulated therein. This measure will vary inversely with the number of letters treated conjointly within the analysis. In English, for example, the likelihood of occurrence of Q and U in sequence is considerably higher than the combined likelihoods of Q and U occurring independently. Thus the average information content of language analyzed by pairs of symbols is lower than that of the same language analyzed by isolated symbols, and in general the more symbols treated jointly for purposes of analysis, within practicable limits, the lower the information measure attached to the language as a whole. Calculations by Shannon suggest that the information content of English is roughly 4 bits on the average for each letter taken individually, but only about 3 bits per letter taken in triads, and only about 1 bit per letter when the entire context of the English expression is taken into account.[14]

In themselves these facts indicate the disparity between information in the technical sense and meaning. Whereas letters generally convey more information separately than in sequence, individual letters in a natural language generally convey no meaning at all. Moreover, a sequence of letters without interpretation in the natural language would thereby be devoid of meaning but could convey a high measure of information in the technical sense. Finally, two letters occurring with about the same frequency in a natural language, such as R and S in English, might combine with the same letters to form expressions of approximately the same information content in bits but with entirely different meanings, such as 'rat' and 'sat.'

INFORMATION CONTENT A PRECONDITION OF MEANING

The basic positive relationship between technical information and meaning is that the former is a necessary but not sufficient condition of the latter. If a channel cannot transmit specific symbol sequences unambiguously, it is not capable of conveying semantically meaningful messages. But the fact that a channel is capable of conveying information in the sense of unambiguous (not necessarily error-free) symbol transmission does not in itself guarantee that every or any sequence of symbols conveyed through that channel will be meaningful. The difference between information theory and semantics in this respect is the difference between the study of the conditions for the communication of any message whatsoever and the study of the content of particular messages.

INFORMATION THEORY AND SEMANTICS

Although communication of meaning is not reducible to communication of information in bits, parallels exist between the two processes which should be instructive to both the semanticist and the linguist. Communication of information begins with the selection of signal sequences out of a field of possible sequences and ends with the interpretation of those signals as represented at the other end of the transmission line. Communication of meaning begins with the selection of particular words out of a field of possible word sequences and ends with the interpretation of these words as represented to the recipient of the message. In both instances interpretation is a form (not the same form) of decoding, and successful reception of the message form is dependent upon correct decoding of its content.

Conditions to be met for successful communication of information in bits include the relative dominance of signal over noise, but even when noise is extreme the message can be salvaged if it involves sufficient redundancy. Similarly conditions for the successful transfer of meaning in word sequences include adherence to rules of grammar, but even with bad grammar the meaning of a message often can be detected from meaning relationships or redundancy among terms. Insofar as linguistics deals with the grammatical structure of communication, it deals with structures which keep our verbal messages free from the noise of nonsensical and hence uninterpretable locutions. And insofar as semantics deals with meaning relationships it deals with redundancies or overlaps in meaning which provide the basis for logical relationships among terms. The parallel here is limited. Yet it is pertinent to observe that the reason 'John is a man' entails 'John is mortal,' for example, is that 'man' occurring in the same predicative context as 'mortal' makes the latter term superfluous. 'John is a man' entails 'John is mortal' because 'man' conveys more information semantically than is conveyed by 'mortal' alone.

Further elucidation of the relationship between technical information and meaning is a philosophic problem of major importance, but one toward which few definitive contributions have yet been made.

ARTIFICIAL INTELLIGENCE

Biologists and behavioral scientists have been attracted to cybernetics particularly by the way in which it seems to remove some of the mystery from the distinction between living and nonliving systems.[15] Wiener's motivation in coining the term 'cybernetics' was to provide a common rubric for discussion of communication and control problems which arise alike in electrical engineering, physiology, and computer technology.[16] Problems in the theory of governors and other negative feedback mechanisms thus were viewed, along with problems of excitation and inhibition in neurology and problems of discrimination and learning in psychology, as problems calling for particular applications of general principles in the theory of control. These principles submit in part to more general formalization within information theory. The unity of cybernetics from the beginning, therefore, rested upon a dismissal of what appears different between living and nonliving systems and upon an emphasis of respects in which they appear comparable or the same.

Early cybernetical mechanisms developed by Walter[17] and Ashby[18] showed that machines can be made capable of goal-directed, or "purposive," adaptation to a changing environment. Work with pattern-recognition and game-playing mechanisms in the late 1950's[19] demonstrated that computer-based mechanical systems can be made capable of self-adaptive, or "learning," behavior. And some recent work by Wiener[20] and others has shown that machines are theoretically possible which even can reproduce themselves in other machines capable of the same functions. Thus it is no longer feasible to claim, at least without considerable qualification, that capability for reproduction, learning or purposive behavior is a discriminating mark of living against nonliving systems.

Of more concern to philosophers in most modern traditions, however, is the distinction between mental and nonmental behavior. The most philosophically significant among recent developments in man-machine studies, therefore, have been various computer-based mechanical systems capable of behavior which in the human being would be considered mental activity. Notable among these are machines for playing checkers and chess, machines capable of proving mathematical and logical theorems, pattern-recognition mechanisms, and mechanical systems for aesthetic creation, all of which fall under the general title "artificial intelligence."

GAME-PLAYING MECHANISMS

Computer programs exist which can compete advantageously with master checker players, and chess probably will submit eventually to automation in the same fashion.[21] Even now computers can be programmed to play better than an elementary game of chess. No gamesmanship here survives, however, for in the playing procedure of the computer each move is made according to specific rules and criteria of merit. Good moves are distinguished from bad according to adjustable values assigned to each piece and to each of its possible positions on the board. The computer's procedure at each stage of play is to trace out the consequences of each possible move in terms of the most likely responses of the opponent, and the move finally selected at each stage of play is the one most likely to leave the computer's pieces in good position at some later stage in the game. Since there are enormously many moves and countermoves at any except the final moments of play, the computer can examine only a few moves ahead and often requires considerable time to make its choice. Each juncture of the game, however, has its best possible move, and the problem of finding this move reduces to a matter of calculating speed and available time. This and the fact that game-playing programs can be made capable of self-improvement through experience provide a reasonable basis for predicting that computers some day will completely master the game of chess.

THEOREM-PROVING MECHANISMS

The object of a proof in mathematics or logic, whether achieved by mechanical or human means, is to proceed from a given sequence of symbols to a specific final sequence of symbols in such a way that each step follows from previous steps according to specific rules for symbol manipulation. The original sequence is the set of axioms and definitions; the final sequence is the theorem proved; the several steps in between collectively are the proof that the theorem follows from the axioms and definitions according to appropriate rules of inference. Given a specific set of symbols as axioms and definitions, to be manipulated according to specific rules, there is a set of specific formulae which could result from these manipulations. The task of the theorem-proving mechanism is to isolate at each stage those consequences of its previously acquired formulae which bring it closer to its stipulated goal. If the desired conclusion in a particular instance follows from the original formulae, there is at least one string of formulae derivable from these which constitutes the proof. To find these formulae and to order them into an appropriate string is to construct a proof that the desired theorem follows from the original axioms and definitions. In the more interesting instances in which the set of possible consequences from the original formulae is infinite, however, this task is achievable by mechanical means only if some method is available for rejecting wholesale all but a few of the more promising possibilities. Thus the human challenge in programming a theorem-proving system is one basically of providing routines to accomplish this winnowing process in a manageable number of steps—or of providing instructions by which the machine can discover and improve upon its own routines in the process of application.

Although mechanical theorem-proving presents problems more severe than those of mechanical chess, some results are already at hand. One program, for example, has been able to prove in less than three minutes the entire list of over 200 theorems in the propositional calculus of *Principia Mathematica*.[22] The program was able to prove also a theorem within the propositional calculus for which the authors of *Principia* had considered the predicate calculus necessary.[23] This counts as an original proof in the best sense of the term.

PATTERN-RECOGNITION AND CREATIVITY

Mechanical character recognition is among the more practical applications of the computer's mindlike abilities. Systems to read printed letters and numbers currently are on the market, and some success has been achieved in preparing computers to recognize letters scrawled by the casual penman.[24] The Postal Department of the United States of America already is using electronic scanning devices to sort mail by Zip Code, and the day probably is not far off when most governmental and business records will be both collected and stored by entirely mechanical means. Comparable progress being made in the mechanical recognition of spoken words soon should make possible mechanical stenographic devices and other systems in which human beings communicate with machines just as they communicate with other human beings.

Among tasks of more immediate human interest currently undertaken by computers is the composition of music and poetry. Although results thus far tend to be of curious rather than aesthetic worth, some computer compositions of music have been copyrighted and published.[25]

PHILOSOPHIC ISSUES

Given the ability of machines to learn, act purposively, and perform tasks which with the human agent require mental skills, it is unavoidable that the question arise whether man himself is anything more than a cybernetical system, constructed of organic rather than inorganic parts. Whereas in the seventeenth and eighteenth centuries mechanism was a strictly theoretical issue, technologists today are debating seriously the practical problems of constructing robots comparable in essential respects to human beings. The question of the significance of artificially intelligent mechanical systems is one of the most pressing philosophic issues of the present day. Some philosophers maintain that recent developments in technology, physiology, and physical science show that the human nervous system with the mental behavior it supports is essentially physical in nature,[26] whereas others claim to be able to prove that there are essential differences between men and machines.[27] More conservative is the view that not enough is known about either men or machines to justify an unqualified answer to the questions of physicalism and mechanism.

MECHANISM

Mechanism may be represented by the thesis (M)

that all men are machines. Arguments both for and against mechanism, on the basis of cybernetic considerations, owe their persuasiveness to the logical relations between M and the thesis (A) that machines can do everything men can do. Although M entails A, the converse does not hold, for it is possible that men and machines do the same things but do them in irreducibly different ways. Since M entails A, however, the negation of A entails the negation of M. This latter entailment provides an argument form which, if successfully used, could establish the falsehood of the mechanistic thesis.

Mechanism would be shown false if it were shown merely that *some* men are not machines. Opponents of M, however, typically would not be satisfied merely to establish its negation but would be concerned further to argue that its contrary is true. Now to show that *no* men are machines it would not be sufficient to show merely that A is false in that there are some things *some* men can do which no machine can do. The contrary of M could be established with regard to A only if A is shown false in that there are some things *all* men can do which no machine can do. One of the most prominent attempts to defeat M by philosophic argumentation in this form has been to argue that since all men but no machines are capable of consciousness, no men are machines. Scriven, for instance, has argued[28] that the presence of or capacity for consciousness provides a criterion by which men can be definitively distinguished from all possible mechanisms.

This particular argument is not an effective instance of the form 'not-A, therefore not-M' for at least two reasons. First, consciousness is not something men do, but rather something men are or are not. Thus to point out that men but not machines are conscious is not to point out something men but not machines can do. A more serious weakness in the argument from consciousness lies in the fact that neither the presence nor the absence of consciousness can serve as exclusive criterion either for the presence or for the absence of any other characteristic in a particular thing. This is true because the presence and absence of consciousness are indicated only on the basis of other behavioral characteristics which themselves fall under A as formulated above. The only way a particular individual can be determined to be conscious is with reference to his observable behavior. If the requisite behavior were absent in all machines but present in all men, then indeed it could be concluded that M is false; but this conclusion would be based on the negation of A reflecting the absence of this behavior and would in no way depend upon the presence of consciousness in men thereby inferred, nor upon its supposed absence in machines. Although it may be true that machines will never be conscious, the belief that this is so arises from the belief that no machines are men, rather than vice versa. Since there is no way the absence of consciousness in machines could be established independently of other behavioral characteristics falling under A, there is no way in which M could be made to stand or fall on considerations of consciousness alone.

To the objection that consciousness is a matter of inner awareness, not of external behavior, and that since machines *in fact* cannot be conscious, machines cannot be men, the reply is simply that the factuality of the claim that machines cannot be conscious, although debatable, is not here in issue. What has been pointed out is that any considerations which provide evidence for the absence of consciousness in machines themselves justify the rejection of M, so that the question of consciousness becomes irrelevant. To the subsequent objection that it is perverse even to honor the possibility that machines might be conscious, the reply is that some machines certainly are conscious if M is true, and hence that to reject this possibility a priori is simply to beg the question against M from the outset, a move devoid of philosophic interest.

Another argument of the form 'not-A, therefore not-M' frequently discussed in recent literature is one which relies upon Gödel's proof that for any formal system capable of producing the truths of arithmetic there is a true formula which cannot be deduced from the axioms of the system.[29] This proof turns upon the fact that for every such system there can be expressed in appropriate notation a formula which is true if and only if that formula is not demonstrable within the system. It follows deductively that if the system is consistent that particular formula cannot be demonstrated within the system. It can be shown by informal reasoning, however, that this particular formula is true. Thus for every consistent system capable of producing the truths of arithmetic there is a statement which people reasoning about the system can show to be true but which cannot be proved within the system itself.

The application of Gödel's proof to the "man-machine" problem rests upon the conception that being a machine is tantamount to being representable as a formal system. The initial states of the machine and of its environment correspond to the axioms of the formal system, its invariant operations to the definitions, its operational procedures to rules of inference, and the results of its operation upon its input to the theorems which follow in the formal system. The argument proceeds with the contention that, although no formal system, and hence no machine, can produce its own Gödelian formula as true, any rational human being in principle can produce as true the Gödelian formula of any machine.[30] The conclusion is that there is at least one thing which in principle all men but no machines can do, from which it follows that no men are machines.

This argument is clearly infirm in its presumption that all men, being in principle rational, can follow Gödel's argument and produce as true the Gödelian formula of every machine. In point of fact there is not even one man who can produce as true the Gödelian formula of every machine, and there is probably not even one man who can produce the required formula for even one nontrivial machine. Apart from matters of fact, however, the argument begs the very question it is intended to settle. Necessarily, any given man either has a Gödelian formula or does not. Further, all and only machines or systems representable as machines have Gödelian formulae, since for all but only such systems are there rules for formulating the expressions from which Gödelian formulae are derived. Now if that man has no Gödelian formula, it is false to say that he can produce his own Gödelian formula as true. In this case, neither man nor machine can produce its own Gödelian formula as true, and no essential difference has been shown between them.[31] If, on the other hand, a man does have a Gödelian formula, that man either is a machine or is representable as a machine, since only such systems have Gödelian formulae. In neither instance, then, has an essential difference between man and machine been established by the argument. It is likely that no men have Gödelian formulae, but as with consciousness the belief that this is so follows from and does not itself justify the belief that no men are machines.

Although the opponent of mechanism has in the relationship between A and M a potentially powerful argument form, no particular argument of this form has been produced which establishes definitively that both A and consequently M are false.

Some perhaps will deem it perverse even to attempt to demonstrate that machines cannot do everything men can do. From an uncritical viewpoint, indeed, it seems obvious that machines not only are insentient, but moreover are incapable among other things of fear, hope, altruism, and love. Thus it might be objected that mechanism is clearly false, apart from considerations like those above, and that the question of its possible truth ought not to be raised seriously in the first place.

The mechanist's response to this objection reveals the considerable dialectical strength of his position. The only requirement for the eventual mechanical performance of any human act, he will argue, is that the act be precisely explicated with reference both to the antecedent conditions upon which it ensues (the input) and to the result achieved in response to these conditions (the output).[32] Thus, for example, the necessary conditions for a theorem-proving program are merely the complete and precise specification of the initial formulae and rules of inference with reference to which the proof is to be constructed, and of the desired theorem with which the proof is to terminate. Similarly, for any aspect of human behavior the only necessary condition in principle for its eventual mechanization is that it be well enough understood to permit precise and detailed statements of its input and output characteristics. The task then of constructing a machine which will accomplish the specified output given the input in question is one merely of technical skill and good fortune. This being the case, the mechanist will argue, the claim that people can do things machines cannot results from confusion and from exploitation of the fact that we do not understand clearly the behavior we mistakenly assume to be uniquely human.

Given the relationship between A and M noted, the mechanist, unlike his opponent, has no way of proving his thesis with reference to things men and machines may or may not be able to do. Yet his dialectical position remains impressively strong. His opponent, the mechanist can argue, will never be able to cite a human act which shows conclusively that no men are machines. For any act of which all men are capable, either the act is or is not clearly understood. If it is not clearly understood, then no clear meaning can be attached to the claim that all men but no machines can accomplish it; and if it is clearly understood, the mechanist will argue, then in principle instructions can be given for its mechanical reproduction. The only effective response to this dilemma by the mechanist's opponent would be to show that there are human acts which can be clearly understood without being understood in terms of input-output characteristics. Whether this can be shown without begging the question against mechanism is an issue not yet resolved.

The dialectical strength of the mechanist position is not a conclusive argument for the truth of mechanism. This discussion shows only that the remarkable advances in artificial intelligence over the past decade do not in themselves alter the philosophic status of the mechanist thesis. Mechanism remains a matter of philosophic persuasion and has not been altered into an issue admitting definitive settlement by empirical considerations.

PHYSICALISM AND DETERMINISM

The thesis (A) that machines can do everything men can do is sometimes cited in arguments, inspired by cybernetics, to support the philosophic theses of physicalism and determinism.[33] It remains to examine logical relationships between A and the assertions, respectively, (P) that only physical things, or matter, exist in the universe, and (D) that all events, including all human activities, are determined in their occurrence by sufficient causes. It will be shown that neither P nor D either implies or is implied by A. In the context of information theory, moreover, A suggests the falsehood of D.

If only physical things exist in the universe, and both men and machines exist in the universe, then both men and machines are entirely physical things. But men and machines might be physical things of entirely different types, as are machines, stones, and radiation fields. If men and machines are physical things of different types, then there may be modes of behavior within the capabilities of one but not the others, just as some machines but no stones are capable of transforming electrical directly into kinetic energy. Thus it is compatible with P that A be false.

If A is true, on the other hand, then possibly either (1) men and machines do everything they do in common in the same fashion and according to the same explanatory principles, or (2) men and machines perform some common acts in different fashions, not to be explained according to the same scientific principles. If (1), and the explanatory principles are mechanistic, then P is true as well as A. If (2), and the principles only according to which some human acts can be explained are not mechanistic, then P is false even though A is true. Thus it is compatible with A that P be false. P, consequently, neither entails nor is entailed by A. It follows that cybernetics, insofar as A represents its central claim of philosophic interest, has no new lessons of logical necessity to teach about the old issue of physicalism.

Cybernetics, however, has perhaps unexpected consequences for determinism. An event is determined by sufficient causes, by definition, if and only if there are antecedent events the occurrence of which conjointly render its occurrence 100 per cent probable. Thesis D accordingly asserts that all events, including all human activities, are rendered 100 per cent probable by antecedent events. It is compatible with D, however, that the history of causally interconnected events antecedent to human acts of a given sort include sufficient conditions for the occurrence of such acts, but that sufficient conditions for such acts are never found among the antecedent events of any mechanical activity. Thus D is compatible with the denial of A. Thesis A, on the other hand, likewise is compatible with the denial of D, since it might be that neither men nor machines are determined in their behavior by antecedent events. Thus D neither entails nor is entailed by the cybernetic thesis A.

An interesting consequence of Wiener's original conception of cybernetics, to the contrary, is its implicit rejection of determinism with regard both to human and to mechanical activity. Cybernetics studies communication not only among men, but also between men and machines themselves.[34] A requirement for the communication of information from sender to receiver, as described, is that the sender be capable of choice among possible message states in such a way that indication of a particular message state is more probable, from the receiver's viewpoint,[35] after than before the sender's choice. If, contrariwise, D is true, then no act of the sender and no indication of his act will be more probable after than before its occurrence. Thus a behaving system, whether human or mechanical, which is completely determined in all its activity according to D is incapable of originating information and hence is incapable of communication in the sense pertinent to Wiener's study of cybernetics.

These remarks do not constitute a definitive

refutation of determinism, for it remains possible that neither men nor machines are capable of communication in the sense pertinent to cybernetics. Since it is highly likely as a point of fact, however, that men at least are capable of communication in this sense, cybernetics renders determinism in human behavior a highly unlikely thesis.

NOTES

1. The term 'cybernetics' has not been universally accepted by mathematicians and engineers in this country, who often prefer to speak instead of information theory and the theory of feedback and control. Use of the term here does not reflect a decision one way or another regarding those issues which disincline many specialists from adopting 'cybernetics' as a technical term.

2. R. Hartley, "Transmission of Information," *Bell System Technical Journal,* 7 (1928), 535–563.

3. C. Shannon, "A Mathematical Theory of Communication," *Bell System Technical Journal,* 27 (1948), 379–423, 623–656.

4. N. Wiener, *Cybernetics* (New York: The Technology Press and John Wiley & Sons, Inc., 1948; 2nd ed., Cambridge, Mass,: M.I.T. Press).

5. L. Brillouin, *Science and Information Theory* (New York: Academic Press, 1956).

6. An informal development of the concept of the bit as a measure of information may be found in Chap-

ter 11 of K. M. Sayre, *Recognition: A Study in the Philosophy of Artificial Intelligence* (Notre Dame: University of Notre Dame Press, 1965).

7. *Loc. cit.*

8. *Loc. cit.*

9. L. Szilard, "Über die Entropieverminderung in einem thermodynamischen System bei Eingriffen intelligenter Wesen," *Zeitschrift für Physik*, 53 (1929), 840-856.

10. N. Wiener, *The Human Use of Human Beings: Cybernetics and Society* (Boston: Houghton Mifflin Co., 1950; 2nd ed. rev., Garden City, New York: Doubleday & Co., Inc., 1954), p. 21.

11. W. Weaver, "Recent Contributions to the Mathematical Theory of Communication" in C. Shannon and W. Weaver, *The Mathematical Theory of Communication* (Urbana: University of Illinois Press, 1949), p. 116; Y. Bar-Hillel, "An Examination of Information Theory," *Philosophy of Science*, 22 (1955), 96; L. Brillouin, *op. cit.*, p. 9; F. Tillman and B. Russell, "Language, Information, and Entropy," *Logique et Analyse*, 30 (1965), 126.

12. *Ibid.*

13. *Op. cit.*

14. C. Shannon, "Prediction and Entropy of Printed English," *Bell System Technical Journal*, 30 (1951), 50–64.

15. F. George, *Cybernetics and Biology* (Edinburgh: Oliver and Boyd, 1965), p. 1.

16. Wiener, *Cybernetics*, p. 11.

17. W. Walter, *The Living Brain* (New York: Norton & Co., 1953).

18. W. Ashby, *Design for a Brain* (London: Chapman & Hall, 1952).

19. O. Selfridge, "Pandemonium: A Paradigm for Learning" in *Mechanisation of Thought Processes,* Blake and Uttley, eds. (London: Her Majesty's Stationery Office, 1959), 1, 513–526.

20. N. Wiener, "On Learning and Self-Reproducing Machines," Supplementary Chapter IX, 2nd ed., *Cybernetics* (Cambridge, Mass.: M.I.T. Press).

21. N. Wiener, *God and Golem, Inc.* (Cambridge, Mass.: M.I.T. Press, 1964), pp. 22ff.

22. H. Wang, "Towards Mechanical Mathematics," *IBM Journal of Research and Development,* 4 (1960), 2–22.

23. *Ibid.,* p. 9.

24. The best available review of this work is in "Cursive Script Recognition," Part III of "Machine Recognition of Human Language," *Spectrum* (May, 1965), 104–116. See also K. M. Sayre, *Recognition: A Study in the Philosophy of Artificial Intelligence.*

25. L. Hiller and L. Isaacson, *Experimental Music* (New York: McGraw-Hill Book Co., Inc., 1959); L. Hiller and R. Baker, "Computer Cantata: A Study in Compositional Method," *Perspectives of New Music,* 3 (1964), 62–90.

26. J. Smart, *Philosophy and Scientific Realism* (London: Routledge & Kegan Paul, 1963); J. Culbertson, *The Minds of Robots* (Urbana: University of Illinois Press, 1963); H. Feigl, "The 'Mental' and the 'Physical'," *Minnesota Studies in the Philosophy of Science,* 2 (Minneapolis: University of Minnesota Press, 1958), 370–497.

27. J. Lucas, "Minds, Machines and Gödel," *Philosophy* (1961), 112–126; M. Scriven, "The Compleat Robot: A Prolegomena to Androidology," *Dimensions*

of Mind, S. Hook, ed. (New York: Collier Books, 1960), pp. 113–133.

28. M. Scriven, "The Mechanical Concept of Mind," *Mind,* 62 (1953), 230–240.

29. K. Gödel, "Über formal unentscheidbare Sätze der Principia Mathematica und verwandter Systeme," *Monatschefte für Mathematik und Physik,* 38 (1931), 173–198.

30. See the opening few paragraphs of Lucas, "Minds, Machines and Gödel."

31. The reason no man can produce as true a Gödelian formula representing his structure as a formal system, in this instance, is different of course from the reason no machine can do likewise. The point of the argument is that inability to produce such a formula does not *in itself* constitute a difference between men and machines. The further difference regarding reasons for this inability with men and machines, respectively, is equivalent when stated with the conclusion of the argument to the effect that no men are machines, and hence cannot with circularity be introduced as evidence within the argument itself.

32. D. MacKay, "Mindlike Behaviour in Artefacts," *British Journal for the Philosophy of Science,* 2 (1951–52), 105–121.

33. Smart, *op. cit.,* pp. 109ff.

34. Wiener, *The Human Use of Human Beings,* p. 16.

35. The expression 'from the receiver's viewpoint' does not refer to what the receiver "sees" or "believes" about the message state or states indicated by the sender. The receiver, indeed, need not be a person, or any agent capable of "seeing" or "believing" in any sense whatever. Nor does the expression mean "relative

to the receiver as such." The transmission of information from point A to point B in a communication system is a matter of an increase in probability of indication of a message state or states at A insofar as such probabilities can be determined relative to point B. The expression above thus should be read as referring to what is determinable regarding the message state or states selected at the source relative to the point in the system occupied by the receiver. The argument which follows relies upon the claim that any event at any stage in a completely determined system is 100 per cent probable relative to any former stage in the system.

II. Information Theory

INFORMATION, MACHINES, AND MEN*

J. L. Massey

INTRODUCTION

THE TITLE OF THIS ESSAY SUGGESTS A SUBJECT so vast that it is hardly necessary to state we shall not be aiming at an exhaustive treatment of it. Rather it shall be our task to examine machines and men from only one aspect, namely, their ro'es in the total process of communication. Our major tool will be the relatively new science of information theory. This science has met with impressive success in its application to the technological phases of the process of communication, but we shall be employing its methods in an arena where their validity is open to serious objections. The reader is advised to establish for himself the reasonableness (or lack thereof) of our methods and conclusions.

Most of the arguments herein are of a dual nature. In the first place, as much of the discussion as possible will be conducted at the technical level where the hypotheses and deductive steps are explicit. Then the technical discussion will be examined for its bearing upon ethical or philosophical matters. It is in this second stage that our arguments will merit the closest possible scrutiny of the reader, both because of the dangers inherent in making the transition from the technical to the philosophical and also because the latter area is the more significant one for us as human beings.

INFORMATION THEORY

Information theory might be defined as the science of messages, since it aims at a numerical formulation of laws which govern the generation, transmission, and reception of messages or "information." Since 1925 there have been sporadic attempts among scientists to devise a quantitative measure of information. This goal was finally achieved satisfactorily by Dr. Claude E. Shannon, then of the Bell Telephone Laboratories. Shannon's paper[1] was immediately recognized as a classic work and resulted overnight in the establishment of information theory as a discipline in its own right. Such was the interest and so many the avenues opened by this new science that more than a thousand technical papers were published in this new field within five years. Yet so thorough was the work of Shannon that there has as yet been no development within information theory for which the seed is not readily visible in his original paper. It is quite interesting, and possibly more than a coincidence of genius, that Shannon has also been accorded the honor of founding a second new discipline. His master's dissertation at the Massachusetts Institute of Technology contained the first application of Boolean algebra to the study of electrical relay circuits. This work led to the establishment of the now very extensive field of switching theory, including the logical design of computers. Besides sharing a common founder, information theory and switching theory have many close connections, and advances in the two fields are often made along parallel lines.

Before we can discuss information theory at the technical level, it will be necessary to have some understanding of probability theory, since this is the branch of mathematics which supplies information theory with its basic vocabulary. As mathematics, probability theory is a consistent and well-developed body. As regards its interpretation, however, the issue is far from settled, and this same ambiguity of interpretation can be expected in information theory. For instance, when we say that the probability is one-half that an unbiased coin will turn up heads, what do we really mean? Is there a basic randomness in coin tossing, or is "probability" just a way of expressing our ignorance of some of the factors in a deterministic situation? Do we mean that the fraction of "heads" would inevitably approach one-half if we conducted an unlimited number of repetitions of the coin-tossing experiment, that is, does the probability express a certain physical law governing many repetitions of the same situation? These are thorny philosophical questions, and we shall not be able to dodge them entirely in what follows.[2]

With an event x we associate at the mathematical level a probability $P(x)$ which is some number between 0 and 1 inclusive. The symbol 'x' might designate the event that a coin will turn up "heads" —in which case we generally choose $P(x) = 0.5$, unless we have some reason to suspect that the coin has been doctored. In the relative frequency interpretation, $P(x)$ is supposed to be the fraction of times one would expect the event x to occur in endlessly many repetitions of the experiment. But it is difficult to apply this interpretation to intrinsically one-time events such as the event of the Yankees winning the pennant in 1967, and it appears impossible to make a relative frequency interpretation of the probability of such an event as that Fermat's famous last theorem is false. We shall reject the relative frequency interpretation in favor of a more subjective interpretation—which, unfortunately, is not without problems of its own. Our interpretation is that the reciprocal of $P(x)$ is the odds that an observer would place on the occurrence of x in a bet which he judged to be fair, that is, should x occur, he would demand a payoff of $\frac{1}{P(x)}$ for each dollar he had wagered on x. For instance, in an even bet where $P(x) = 0.5$ he would expect to receive two dollars (his own dollar plus a dollar of profit) if he had wagered one. Against such an interpretation it can be objected that $P(x)$ now depends upon the observer as well as the event x itself and that $P(x)$ will reflect the "information" available to the observer. As we shall see, this is very much the manner in which "information" is considered in information theory.

According to information theory the occurrence of an event y provides an amount of information about the occurrence of an event x which is given by the formula

$$(1) \qquad I(x; y) = \log_2 \frac{P(x/y)}{P(x)}$$

where $P(x/y)$ is the probability assigned to x after y has been observed to occur. The base of the logarithm is arbitrary but is usually chosen to be 2, as it is written in equation (1), in which case the unit of information is called the "bit." Equation (1) has a very simple interpretation. If the observance of y doubles the probability of x (that is, halves the odds we would place on x), then y provides + 1 bit of information about x. Similarly, if y halves the probability of x (doubles the odds we would place on x), then y provides − 1 bit of information about x. If the probability of x is unchanged by the observance of y, then y provides no information at all about x.

In order to make x a certainty, (that is, to make $P(x/y) = 1$), equation (1) shows that y would have to provide

$$(2) \qquad \log_2 \frac{1}{P(x)} = -\log_2 P(x)$$

bits of information about x. Letting X denote the ensemble $x_1, x_2, \ldots, x_n$ of n possible events, one and only one of which actually occurs, then with the aid of (2) we find that the average amount of information required to make one of the events in x a certainty is

$$(3) \qquad H(X) = -\sum_{i=1}^{n} P(x_i) \log_2 P(x_i)$$

and is a measure of the a priori *uncertainty* of the ensemble X. This quantity is also called the *entropy* of the ensemble X, by analogy to statistical thermodynamics where the same formula occurs. If X is an ensemble of only two events, then $H(X) \leq 1$ bit with equality when and only when the two events are equiprobable. Thus 1 bit of information represents that amount of information required to distinguish between two equiprobable alternatives. Similarly, 2 bits of information suffice to distinguish among $2^2 = 4$ equally probable alternatives, 3 bits among $2^3 = 8$ alternatives, and so forth. Put in a slightly different way, 1 bit of information suffices to halve the number of alternatives, assuming all alternatives to be equally likely.

Suppose now that X represents the vocabulary of some information source, and that once each second an event from X is selected according to the probability distribution $P(x_i)$, independently of the events already selected. According to information theory, the "information rate" of such a source is $H(X)$ bits per seconds. But the uncertainty $H(X)$ will be zero when and only when one of the events in X has probability one and the others all have probability zero. In more familiar terms this is analogous to saying that a speaker whose next word can always be anticipated is producing no information for his listener. It is important to note that there is no underlying assumption that the information source possesses intelligence, although this possibility is not excluded. Reduced to its simplest terms, we might say that an object is an information source with respect to an observer when and only when its output X is not completely predictable by the observer. The same object can then produce information for some observers but not for others. For instance, a road sign might yield much information to a stranger to its vicinity and none at all to a local resident.

The average amount of information provided by an event y about an event in the ensemble X is given by the formula

$$(4) \qquad I(X; y) = \sum_{i=1}^{n} P(x_i/y) \, I(x_i; y)$$

With the aid of equation (1) and the inequality

$$\log_2 W \leq \frac{(W-1)}{\ln 2}$$

where 'ln 2' denotes the naperian logarithm of 2, it follows from (4) that

(5) $\qquad I(X; y) \geq 0$

This inequality is consistent with our intuitive notion that on the whole there is some positive amount of information to be garnered from every event.

If y is a member of the ensemble $Y = \{y_1, y_2, \ldots y_m\}$, then the average information provided by an event in Y about an event in X is given by

(6) $\qquad I(X; Y) = \sum_{j=1}^{m} P(y_j) \, I(X; y_j)$

and hence must also be nonnegative. Equation (6) can also be written

(7) $\qquad I(X; Y) = H(X) - H(X/Y)$

where $H(X/Y)$ is the average over the ensemble Y of the uncertainty

(8) $\qquad H(X/y_j) = -\sum_{i=1}^{n} P(x_i/y_j) \log_2 P(x_i/y_j)$

The expression for $H(X/y_j)$ in (8) differs from that for $H(X)$ in (3) only in that the a posteriori probabilities $P(x_i/y_j)$ replace the a priori probabilities $P(x_i)$. Thus (7) expresses the intuitively pleasing notion that the amount of information provided by Y about X is just equal to the amount by which knowledge of Y reduces the uncertainty of X.

At this point it seems appropriate to make some distinction between information in the technical sense we are employing and "meaning." We note in the first place that there is no reason why the X and Y ensembles in the above discussion must be distinct. When X and Y are chosen to be the same ensemble, then (7) reveals that

$$(9) \qquad I(Y; Y) = H(Y)$$

Suppose that Y is the vocabulary of a madman. Then (9) gives a sense in which the speech of a madman conveys information, but it is information only about the speech itself, that is, what would be required to reconstruct his speech. But in the usual sense, we would wish to say that the speech of a madman is meaningless or nearly so. On a formal level it would seem that we are suggesting that $I(X; Y) = 0$, or equivalently that $H(X/Y) = 0$, for ensemble X distinct from Y, when we state that Y is meaningless. Thus meaning seems intimately related to "other-information" [$I(X; Y)$] as opposed to "self-information" [$I(Y; Y)$]. We have dwelt on this point with some emphasis since it has been a common charge against information theory that meaning cannot adequately be taken into account.

In particular, it is frequently cited that since H(Y) is generally greater for a madman than for a sane man, that is, the speech of a madman is less predictable, information theory would hold that the speech of the former contains more information than the latter. Such an interpretation, however, ignores the distinction between self-information and other-information which we have attempted to elucidate.

INFORMATION AND IRREVERSIBILITY

We now turn to our task of applying information theory beyond its usual technical confines. Our first consideration will concern the manner in which information is employed by its recipient, and we shall be led to what seems a basic principle of irreversibility, a principle that is not without ethical overtones.

Consider the simple dichotomous ensemble $X = \{x_1, x_2\}$ of two events, one but only one of which is in effect. For example, x might designate the event that "there is no nuclear warfare in the year 1970," and $1/P(x_1)$ is then the odds that a (somewhat blasé) bettor would ask on this event. The symbol x_2 of course designates the negation of x_1 and has the probability $P(x_2) = 1 - P(x_1)$ since either x_1 or x_2, but not both, must occur. The single number $P(x_1)$ thus suffices to describe the bettor's "state of mind" on the dichotomy X. We might say that he held a strong opinion on X when $P(x_1) = \varepsilon$ or

$P(x_1) = 1-\varepsilon$ where ε is a positive number much less than 1, for example, $\varepsilon = .001$. When $P(x_1) = \varepsilon$ the bettor is almost certain that x_1 is not the case, whereas when $P(x_1) = 1-\varepsilon$ he would be similarly sure that x_1 is the case. Thus ε is a measure of the bettor's doubt about the dichotomy X.

It is interesting to calculate the quantity of information that is required to change the mind of a bettor with a strong opinion on X, that is to find the amount of information $I(X, y)$ provided by an event y which would cause $p(x_1/y) = 1 - p(x_1)$. With the aid of (1) and (4) the amount is readily calculated to be

$$(10) \qquad I(X; y) = -\log_2 \varepsilon$$

(to within a very close approximation). The amount of information given by (10) seems surprisingly small. For instance when $\varepsilon = .001$, that is, when the bettor is willing initially to give 1000 to 1 odds that x_1 is not the case, 10 bits of information from an event y favoring the contrary opinion would suffice to cause the bettor to hold the latter opinion with the same fervor he had originally attached to the former. Even had the original odds been as much as 1,000,000 to 1, only 20 bits of information could change the bettor's mind.

Still more interesting is the question of the amounts of information required to strengthen or to weaken a strong opinion. Suppose that originally $p(x_1) = \varepsilon_1$, whereas the event y causes $p(x_1/y) = \varepsilon_2$, where ε_1 and ε_2 are both small positive frac-tions. When ε_1 is less than ε_2, the bettor's opinion is weakened (his doubt is increased) by observance of y. Similarly $\varepsilon_2 < \varepsilon_1$ implies that the bettor's opinion has been strengthened. Again applying (1) and (4) we find that to a very close approximation

$$(11) \qquad I(X; y) = 1.45\varepsilon_1 + \varepsilon_2 \log_2 \frac{1}{\varepsilon_1}$$

This equation has some rather startling consequences. Whenever $\varepsilon_2 < \varepsilon_1$, that is, whenever y serves to strengthen the bettor's opinion to any degree whatsoever, $I(X; y)$ is very small, much less than 1 bit. On the other hand, when $\varepsilon_1 < \varepsilon_2$, a significant quantity of information is required from y. *The quantity of information required to weaken an opinion is always many times greater than that required to strengthen it.* For instance, the case $\varepsilon_1 = .001$ and $\varepsilon_2 = .000001$ according to (11) requires only about one-fourteenth the information as for the case when $\varepsilon_1 = .000001$ and $\varepsilon_2 = .001$, although the absolute amount of information is still very small in the latter case, namely about .02 bits. But when $\varepsilon_1 = .001 = 10^{-3}$ and $\varepsilon_1 = 10^{-3000}$, not only the ratio of informations is large, namely 7000 to 1, but also a full 10 bits of information are required to weaken the opinion. Such an example may seem rather strained since 10^{-3000} is a very small probability indeed. But if at first it seems unreasonable that a bettor should ever hold an opinion with such a high degree of certainty, we must remind ourselves that (11) shows that when y provided only

.006 bits of information in favor of an opinion he held with the moderate degree of doubt indicated by $\varepsilon_1 = .001$, then the bettor advances to this very high degree of conviction.

The point to this calculation is that the slide toward certainty is a very easy one indeed, whereas the reverse trip is considerably more demanding. As a matter of fact, equation (11) shows that the removal of total conviction, that is, $\varepsilon_1 = 0$, would require from y an infinite amount of information, and hence is impossible. This seems to provide an explanation of why it is useless to reason with a fanatic.

Our investigation has brought to light what appears to be a fundamental fact of irreversibility. To strengthen an opinion always requires less information than to weaken one. The reading of Plato's *Republic* might afford an illustration of this principle. Do we not find Plato's arguments in favor of positions we already hold, such as perhaps that of the immortality of the soul or the need for a king to be a philosopher, much more cogent than his arguments on positions offensive to us, such as the abolition of the family among guardians or the deceptions to be practiced by rulers? Does not this basic irreversibility also show why many generations are required to erase the blight of racial prejudice and why heresies are quick to rise but painfully slow to fall?

On the other hand, may we not also take comfort in the fact that opinions are not too difficult to reverse when they are not held with exceedingly great conviction? This gives hope that an open mind, if mistaken, may without great difficulty be restored to reason. The ethical conclusion seems forced upon us that we must be most zealous in preserving whatever flexibility of opinion that the evidence reaching us allows. The basic irreversibility of the march toward conviction suggests that the wise man will be much more exacting in weighing the evidence in favor of his opinions than in weighing that against them.

TRANSMISSION OF INFORMATION

Perhaps the most celebrated portion of Shannon's theory was his demonstration that every physical channel has a definite numerical capacity for conveying information. Shannon showed that when the rate of information transfer is less than channel capacity, it is possible to "code" the information in such a way that it will reach the receiver with arbitrarily high fidelity. In other words, the probability that the message will be correctly received can be made arbitrarily close to unity. (Some doubt as to correctness must always remain, but this doubt can be made exceedingly small.) The converse of Shannon's theorem is equally significant. If the rate of information transfer exceeds channel capacity, then the surplus information inevitably will be lost in transit. Shannon's theorem is entirely general. It applies to any physical channel, such as the radio channels used to communicate with space vehicles, or to the academic channel between the minds of a professor and his students. It is hardly necessary to add that the numerical value of channel capacity is much more difficult to ascertain for channels of the latter kind than for the former.

To achieve reliable communication thus requires that the source rate be reduced to a point below channel capacity. Let us investigate the two ways that such a reduction can be achieved. Since information in the technical sense is a priori uncertainty, the information rate of a source is just the uncertainty per second of the symbols which it generates. These symbols might be binary numbers in a digital communication system or letters of our own alphabet in human communications. The most obvious way for the source to lower its information rate is to "speak slower," that is, to reduce the number of symbols per second without reducing the uncertainty of each symbol. This is usually the method we use in conversation with someone who has not mastered our language or with a person whose hearing is impaired. Before Shannon this was the only means considered for reducing the source rate in any communication system. But there is a second way to reduce the information rate—namely to generate as many symbols as originally with less uncertainty per symbol. In such an instance the source symbols are not maximally uncertain, but each symbol is determined in large part by the symbols that have gone before and those that follow. Now when a symbol is lost or misinterpreted, it is quite possible that the context will provide clues by which it may be possible to restore or to correct the lost or erroneous symbol.

When the second method of source rate reduction is chosen, the source will be using more symbols than are needed simply to hold the information. A *code* consists of rules by which context is created among the symbols, and the *redundancy* of the code is the percentage of "extra" symbols that result from the creation of context. Redundancy means simply spreading less information over more symbols. The *constraint length* of a code is a measure of the span of symbols over which the context is significant.

The surprising feature of Shannon's theory is that the goal of reliable communication at a rate near channel capacity can be achieved only by the second method of rate reduction, by coding. When the first method is employed, increasing reliability always means further reducing the rate of information transmission, and arbitrarily reliable transmission can be achieved only for a zero rate. Whereas with coding, provided the rate is initially below channel capacity, reliability can be increased indefinitely by increasing the code length without any further sacrifice of information rate.

A recent issue of *Saturday Review* contained the following so-called "paradoxism" which seems most appropriate to our study: "Avoid redundancy, since said repetitive redundancy subjects the hearer to many unnecessary repetitions of phrases repeated over and over again."[3] Is it not surprising then that this same often abused redundancy is the *sine qua non* of reliable communication at high rates of information transfer?

We mentioned earlier that coding (context creation) was not conceived as a way of increasing reliability prior to Shannon. This is not to say that it was never unconsciously used for this purpose. On the contrary, natural languages are for the most part very rich codes for communication purposes. It is quite surprising on first encounter to discover that typical English text has a redundancy of about 80 per cent—that only about one-fifth of the symbols on a page are really necessary to transmit the information.[4] We rely upon the code of English language whenever we capture the information from a page in spite of occasional misprints and our own careless oversights. And it is surely true that we can get the same amount of information more quickly from reading English text than we could from reading an "idealized" language in which every combination of symbols is a valid sentence. On the other hand, it is equally evident that natural language does not attain the goal of extremely reliable communication at high rates of information transfer. The length of the code is probably too short from a purely information-theoretic viewpoint. After all, natural language is employed to a large extent in situations where great reliability is not of paramount importance.

Here we seem to have arrived at a paradox. Shannon's novel idea turns out to have been realized to some extent in human communication as a result of what must have been a haphazard process of language development. Some explanation of this can be deduced from Shannon's work. For Shannon showed that the average behavior of codes selected at random is practically the same as that of an optimum code. Equally remarkable is the fact that for long codes no systematic procedures of encoding have as yet been found which perform as well as the average of all codes. This suggests that attempts to build too much structure into a code end in destroying its error-correcting power. The fact that natural languages are effective codes for communication is probably the result of their haphazard origin as much as anything else.

It seems that one can infer from these ideas some valid principles for human communication. For an example, consider that case in which a teacher has a certain amount of information to convey to his students. Will he not have a better chance of succeeding if, rather than by going slowly with a very compact presentation, he moves along at a fairly rapid rate but weaves in considerable redundancy by examples, illustrations, rewordings, and so forth? Especially where reliability considerations are uppermost, should not a man present his ideas in a context strong enough that misinterpretation of one or more key points will not damage the integrity of the message beyond compare?

As another instance, consider the further development of natural languages themselves. Should we not attempt to employ information-theoretic principles in consciously shaping their future evolution? Perhaps such considerations as we have given here seem too obvious for statement. There does, however, seem to be a tendency to equate redundancy with repugnancy. A clear word of warning is in order that redundancy can be a most beneficial expediency which we ought not be too quick to abandon for more compact alternatives.

GENERATION OF INFORMATION

Having proceeded upstream in the flow of information, we turn our attention now to the manner in which information is generated at the origin. It has seemed appropriate to reserve this subject for the last place because it is here that our conclusions may seem to be most unorthodox. For we hope to show that "intelligence" is unnecessary in the process of information generation, even for information which men find meaningful in a purely human sense. It will be argued that information does not of itself provide clues to its origin, and that information from a mechanical source is all too likely to be construed as having human roots.

We begin by way of illustration. Suppose that one had compiled a long sequence of "yes and no" questions for a human being that are unrelated to one another and for which neither answer is a priori more likely. Our questions might be: "Are you a male?" "Are you above the median height for your sex?" "Are you over 25 years of age?" and so forth. Suppose next we put these questions to a person who is hidden from us within a large black box and who responds by lighting a red lamp on its front to signify no and a green lamp to signify yes. After thirty questions, we might feel we had an extremely good description of our invisible friend. Indeed the probability that two people would answer all thirty questions in the same way is about one in one billion. Finally, suppose that we also had a second identical black box in which was placed a machine that on command would flip a penny and announce "tails" with a green light or "heads" with the red light. The point to be made here is that had the boxes been accidentally switched and had we put our questions to the machine, we would be unable to determine that its responses were not those of a human subject who was honestly answering our questions. In each instance the black box appears as an information source of 1 bit per answer (since the two answers are equiprobable), and moreover in each we attribute the same meaning to the information received —that is, we use the information to adjust our belief as to the sort of human being in the box.

The general situation from an information-theoretic viewpoint appears as follows. An information source is purely and simply any device (man, machine, or other) whose output symbols are not perfectly predictable in advance. Moreover, two information sources with the same output alphabet (the same set of possible output events) and the same probability structure are entirely equivalent and cannot be distinguished. By same probability structure we mean that for both devices, given any specified sequence of past output symbols, the probability that the next output is any prescribed symbol is the same for both sources. This condition was fulfilled in a trivial way in the simple example above by making each output symbol independent of all the preceding ones for both the human being and for the "penny-tossing" machine.

Granted that two information sources can be indistinguishable, it follows that if an observer would attribute meaning to the output of one then he would also attribute meaning to the output of the other if the latter is actually present when he believes the former to be present. It is important to stress the fact that indistinguishability here is meant in a total sense; if two sources are indistinguishable there will not even be means by which one can determine from the output symbols that one or the other is more probably present.

Now it is a very simple matter in principle to construct a device whose output symbols have any prescribed probability structure. From a practical standpoint the device may be too complicated to construct if the probability structure has dependencies over long spans of symbols. The probability structure of any information source, however, can be measured to any desired degree of precision if an adequate observation interval is used. It follows that any information source can be simulated in a way to make the probability that the real and simulated source can be distinguished as small as desired.

We can thus state categorically that it is impossible to devise any sequence of tests that will infallibly, or with high probability, distinguish between the products of human intelligence and those of artificial intelligence. One simply needs (in theory at least) to condition the probability structure of the machine to correspond to that of the human being it is intended to simulate. Thus all attempts to formulate criteria sufficient to establish the presence of qualities such as thought, consciousness, life, and the like are destined to failure. We do not mean to imply that such attempts are without any value, for they may lead computer scientists to devise cleverer and cleverer machines to pass each new test. But this is hardly the intention of the humanists who devise such tests.

When we have discussed these ideas on past occasions, we have frequently encountered the objection that our conclusions have no practical significance. The illustration of the black boxes was so overly simplified as really to be worthless and—granted that our conclusions were correct—a human information source is so complicated that no machine could ever credibly simulate it. A recent journal article[5] describing the ELIZA computer program now in operation at the Massachusetts Institute of Technology presents evidence that such critics are unaware of the existing potential of modern computing machines. The ELIZA (named for the character in *Pygmalion*) is a program which simulates the response of a psychiatrist in the type of conversation employed in psychological analysis. Not only was the simulation credible to one who was unaware he was discoursing with a machine, but "Some subjects have been very hard to convince that ELIZA (with its present script) is *not* human [original italics]." Moreover, "ELIZA shows, if nothing else, how easy it is to create and maintain the illusion of understanding, hence perhaps of judgment deserving of credibility. A certain danger lurks there." And it should be added that from all indications the computers and programs of today will look quite primitive in another twenty years.

Our conclusion must be that real information can be generated by machines and that this information can have the attributes we generally posit only for information of a human origin. But this position must not be equated with the conclusion that "machines think" or any other anthropomorphism. It means simply that the output of machines often possesses uncertainty relative to its observer and that such outputs can alter men's beliefs in the state of events in the world. To use a computing machine at all is to concede that one has some uncertainty as to the answer it will generate, and to accept its answer is to alter one's beliefs. In this light men can truly communicate with machines, and as the author of the ELIZA article observed, therein lies a "certain danger." To this danger we now turn our attention.

MAN-MACHINE INTERACTION

If machines can influence our thoughts, then most certainly they can be said to influence our actions. Many of our actions spring from information reaching us from some machine. A barometer may determine whether we take an umbrella as we depart for work, and a computing machine may advise us on the best path for a proposed expressway. It is more obvious, but equally true, that we can also influence the actions of machines. That we cannot do so to a complete extent will shortly become evident.

Until now we have spoken as though there is no difficulty in deciding after examination which objects are men and which are machines. We have noted the difficulty if we are limited to an examination of the communication from an object, but we have assumed that there was no inherent problem in classifying an object if all the information about the object was available. At present we would probably all agree with this, but there are disturbing indications of trouble ahead. There are numerous predictions of machines which "think" and "act" like human beings. A biologist colleague, on the other hand, has remarked categorically and in public that "human beings" soon will be synthesized to order in biological laboratories. The boundary between human beings and artifacts which now seems intuitively so obvious appears in danger of breaking down. This leads us to propose in all seriousness the following inductive definition of a human being based on the notion that at least at this writing the class of human beings is well determined:

Definition: 1. The objects recognized as such at this writing are human beings. 2. Objects produced by biological reproduction from human beings are human beings. 3. Upon the election by majority vote of human beings of a court with jurisdiction in the designation of human beings, any objects declared to be such by this court are human beings. 4. There are no other human beings.

Though there may never arise an urgent need for such a definition, there seems to be some wisdom in preparing for the eventuality beforehand. Moreover, were such a definition to be widely accepted, it could be of some use at the present. For we could then define as a necessary condition for possession of thought, consciousness, and the like, that these be the unique attributes of human beings. When these same concepts are applied to machine behavior, it would then be clear that they should be interpreted only anthropomorphically. Such an agreement could put an end to many senseless disputes between scientists and humanists.

The third point in our definition may be the cause of some alarm to the defenders of human uniqueness. One hopes that it is such as they who would be elected to the court, but there does seem a certain urgency in retaining this much flexibility in our notion of a human being. It is not inconceivable that a machine could be so refined that we should want the machine to hold the office of Secretary of State. Would we not want to treat one who destroyed such a machine maliciously as a murderer?

Having defined precisely what we might mean by a human being, let us return to the phenomenon of man-machine interaction and specifically to the ethical principles that follow from the nature of this interaction. The founder of cybernetics, Norbert Wiener, stated one such principle in the title of his book, *The Human Use of Human Beings*. Another principle follows as a parallel to this one, namely the need to ensure "the mechanical use of machines." Indeed, we are more likely to fail in the latter than in the former. By the mechanical use of machines as an ethical principle, I mean that *we must never permit a machine to make an important decision affecting human beings except under the direction and control with veto rights of human beings.*

One might object that such concerns are frivolous since no machine, even the most complex digital computer, ever does anything that its designer and users, all human beings, do not intend. The answer is that this objection is not valid today, that it will be less valid tomorrow, and as a matter of fact that it can never be valid.

An anecdote will make the point concretely. An acquaintance recently related to me the story of an engineering student who had been hired as a summer programmer by a large manufacturer of digital computers. The student was given the assignment of reviewing some of the company's standard FORTRAN subroutines. In examining the program to compute logarithms, he was surprised (having been well taught that there is no real number which is the logarithm of a negative number) to discover that there was no check to ensure that a number was positive before its logarithm was taken. Upon informing his supervisor of this fact, he was told to insert such a test immediately so as to produce a halt in computation and an appropriate diagnostic message to the user whenever a program asked for the logarithm of a negative number. The next day several programs halted with this diagnostic message—programs which had previously been running and furnishing their users with "information." We can only guess what use such information found.

The modern digital computer is so complex, and becoming more so every day, that it is increasingly difficult to determine whether our instructions to it are what we really intend. The usual practice is to write a program, give it to the computer whose diagnostic routine then informs us of the obvious errors we have made, and subsequently to revise and re-revise our program until it is finally executed with no diagnostics. Then, especially if we have tried a few examples and received the expected answers, we generally conclude that our instructions to the machine are what we had intended. The chance of error in this process is certainly great enough that we must never trust the machine fully. We must always have human intuition standing on guard between the machine and any humanly important implementation of its output in the world.

It might be objected that we have drawn the wrong conclusion, and that our argument shows not that we must stand watch over the output of machines but that we must exercise greater care in the formulation of our inputs to machines. That this latter course of action is not sufficient to guarantee control over machines follows from some well-known results of Turing in the theory of computation. Turing has shown that it is impossible to formulate a test which when applied to an arbitrary computational program with its input data can determine even so little as whether or not the machine will ever come to a halt in its computation. A general safeguarding program is thus impossible.[6] Moreover, the same theory shows there must exist particular programs for which there is no way of telling whether or not they will ultimately halt. How then can we ever expect to retain control over machines if we exercise our control only over their inputs? We shall always need human guardians over their outputs as well.

The urgency of ensuring the mechanical use of machines is greatly increased by the evolution in computing machines which has now reached the stage in which machines are beginning to be equipped with "effector" organs for applying the results of their computation directly to the physical (and human) world. There is great danger that such machines may implement decisions of their own which their makers did not intend.

Should we not have qualms of conscience whenever—as often happens—we hear of proposals to have machines make at least the routine decisions in business, politics, warfare, and even human mating? Even when the risk to humanity seems minimal on the surface, the potential consequences can be quite frightening. For example, the so-called "information explosion" has led information theorists and others to propose information retrieval schemes in which a research worker would furnish the library computer with just a subject title and the machine would deliver to him a list of all the pertinent books and papers. This could certainly be a great boon to future scholars. However, we must never let the machine control *fully* the books we examine for it might exclude all the literature on an opposing position which it "wanted" to hide from us. We must retain the right to demand a particular book whether or not the machine considers it worth our time to read. As our society becomes more and more complex, more and more will machines be called upon to exercise new functions. We must always insist that insofar as it is possible human rights will always take precedence over mechanical considerations.

We cannot expect that the computer scientists themselves will protect us adequately from the dangers of machine invasion of human rights. Not all these scientists have the humanistic insight of the author of the ELIZA article, who recognizes the dangers involved. Incredible as it may seem, a very influential computer scientist is using a similar program at a different university for the actual treatment of mentally disturbed students with virtually no attempt to preserve human control of the process. The danger is clear and present that we will default our human rights too quickly in the cause of technological improvement. The vigilance of all human beings will be needed to preserve those rights.

The proper function of the computing machine is to extend or amplify our human intelligence, to serve us as an "intelligence amplifier." The danger is that amplifiers of any kind, according to the well-known results of feedback analysis, possess the possibility of becoming "oscillators" or independent agents if their outputs also effect their inputs. This is certainly true of computing machines with mechanical effector organs, and it is also true when human beings serve as the effector organs of the machine. The more powerful the amplifier, the greater is the likelihood that it will oscillate, that it will take an independent course, that it will go out of control. Where the effects of loss of control could have grave consequences for the future of man, I plead that we always maintain within the feedback loop a human being who can break the cycle when he deems it necessary.

AFTERTHOUGHT

A survey of this paper finds us in the position of having applied technical theories rather shamelessly in our human world, and then arguing equally shamelessly that these theories show the danger of trusting too much in technical things. Our hope is that this inconsistency has at least been consistent with the principle enunciated by Richard Bellman in 1962 at the Polytechnic Institute of Brooklyn Symposium on the Mathematical Theory of Automata: "If we are to avoid the morass of metaphysics, we must reduce as many concepts as possible to numerical terms. On the other hand, we must face the fact that the most important aspects of human life are intrinsically nonnumerical. Any attempt to ignore this is highly unscientific. In the true intellectual approach, one accepts this fact and copes with it."[7]

NOTES

* This paper is an expanded version of material originally presented in a lecture of the same title on November 14, 1965, at Sacred Heart Seminary in Detroit, Michigan. The author is grateful to Sacred Heart Seminary for permission to publish this material in this volume.

1. C. Shannon and W. Weaver, *The Mathematical Theory of Communication* (Urbana: University of Illinois Press, 1949), containing a reprint of Shannon's 1948 articles which appeared originally in the *Bell System Technical Journal*.

2. A standard technical treatment of probability theory is W. Feller, *An Introduction to Probability Theory and its Applications* (New York: Wiley, 1950). Readers not acquainted with problems in the interpretation of the probability calculus may refer to R. Carnap, "The Two Concepts of Probability," *Philosophy and Phenomological Research*, 5 (1944–45), 513–532, reprinted in *Readings in the Philosophy of Science*, H. Feigl and M. Brodbeck, eds. (New York: Appleton-Century-Crofts, Inc., 1953), and elsewhere.

3. *Saturday Review of Literature*, November 13, 1965, p. 14.

4. Although Shannon at one time estimated the entropy of English at 50 per cent (Shannon and Weaver, *op. cit.*, p. 27), his later estimations suggest 80 per cent as a more accurate approximation. This figure results from an approximate 5 bits per symbol rate for the alphabet free from context and an approximate 1 bit per symbol rate in ordinary English context. See N. Abramson, *Information Theory and Coding* (New

York: McGraw-Hill, 1963), pp. 33–38, and C. Shannon, "Prediction and Entropy of Printed English," *Bell System Technical Journal*, 30 (1951), 50–64.

5. J. Weizenbaum, "ELIZA—A Computer Program for the Study of Natural Language Communication Between Man and Machine," *Communications of the ACM*, 9, 1 (January 1966), 36–43.

6. See M. Davis, *Computability and Unsolvability* (New York: McGraw-Hill, 1958).

7. R. Bellman, "Dynamic Programming, Intelligent Machines, and Self-Organizing Systems," *1962 Polytechnic Institute of Brooklyn Symposium on Mathematical Theory of Automata* (New York: Polytechnic Institute of Brooklyn Press and Interscience), pp. 10–11.

CHOICE, DECISION, AND THE ORIGIN OF INFORMATION

K. M. Sayre

I

1. I WANT TO CONSIDER THE QUESTION whether machines can communicate with people or with other machines, in the sense of 'communicate' pertinent to information theory. My reason for considering this question is not merely to answer it, for I think the answer is clearly affirmative. I wish to show, rather, that the conditions for an affirmative answer require a sharper distinction than usually has been made between the concepts of choice and decision. Information theory, which studies these conditions, thereby provides a wedge by which these concepts can be definitively separated.

2. The technically pertinent question today is

not whether machines can communicate with people or other machines, but rather how machines can be made to communicate more efficiently. Norbert Wiener, introducing the topic of *The Human Use of Human Beings,* remarks:

> It is the thesis of this book that society can only be understood through a study of the messages and the communication facilities which belong to it; and that in the future development of these messages and communication facilities, messages between man and machines, between machines and man, and between machine and machine, are destined to play an ever-increasing part.[1]

As Wiener saw, it is immaterial from the point of view of information theory[2] whether the communication studied is between man and man, man and machine, or among machines solely. The case for the affirmative appears unassailable: of course machines can communicate with people, and with other machines.

But herein lie the seeds of paradox. Strange as it may appear, information theory also provides persuasive reasons for *denying* that machines can communicate at all. To see how this is so, let us briefly review the basic requirements of a communication system.

3. Communication between human beings, by whatever system of language or code, involves a sender, a receiver, and a channel through which the message is conveyed. The sender is the source

of the message, the receiver is its destination, and the channel is the means by which the message remains coherent and articulate in the process of transmission. There are many channels through which people communicate. Consequently, since a message must be properly formulated for conveyance through any given channel, there are many ways in which a message may be formulated or encoded by its human originator. If the channel is a telegraph wire, the message must be encoded in a series of long and short electrical pulses. If the channel is a fluctuating electromagnetic field, the message must be encoded in the form of modulations of a standard carrier frequency. And if the channel is an inscribed writing surface, the message must be represented by marks arranged according to conventions which the writer presumes to share with his potential readers.

In general the requirement for initiating an act of communication is that the sender have at his disposal a range of alternative message states, among which he can choose in a way which indicates the contents of his intended message. Information originates with a choice among alternative message states and with the representation of that choice in a form suitable for transmission through the appropriate channel. Information subsequently is received at the destination when the coded representation is interpreted to indicate the same choice, or series of choices, which it was intended to represent at its origin.

Thus there is a sense in which the act of choice is an essential ingredient of the communication transaction.[3] This requirement, moreover, is a direct consequence of the definition of the unit measure in information theory. Let us trace the outlines of this consequence.

4. Consider a very simple communication system in which the sender (S) is capable of selecting either of two message states (yes and no) for transmission to the receiver (R). If there is equal a priori probability of selecting either message, the actual transmission of either yes or no would convey the same amount of information. Before transmission, the probability of sending yes, for example, is 50 per cent; after transmission, with no error, the probability is 100 per cent. By the same token, R's uncertainty as to the message state transmitted has been decreased from 50 per cent to zero.

The quantity of information required to bring about this decrease in uncertainty is designated 1 bit. It is relatively rare, of course, that a given choice conveys exactly 1 bit of information, since it is relatively rare that a given choice is exactly 50 per cent probable on a priori grounds. If the choice of yes by S were initially only 25 per cent probable, more uncertainty on the part of R would be removed by the reception of yes and more information accordingly would be conveyed by the transmission of that choice. On the other hand, if less uncertainty is removed by the reception of a given message state, as for instance if its initial probability were 75 per cent, then less information would be conveyed by the choice and actual transmission of that state. Information theory has a precise formula expressing the amount of information conveyed by a choice with a given initial probability.[4] For our purposes it is enough to note that the amount of information in bits conveyed by the correct transmission and reception of a given message state is equal to the number of times the initial probability of that state must be doubled to reach 100 per cent.[5]

With this scant introduction to information theory, we are in a position already to see why choice is an essential part of the communication transaction. If S has no choice with regard to a particular message state, it may be because either there is no possibility (that is, zero probability) that he will choose that state or there is no possibility that he will not choose it. In the first instance no information is conveyed by the choice since the choice is never made; in the second no information is conveyed because no uncertainty is removed when an indication of that choice is received. Since there is no communication without conveyance of information, no communication is possible save from a source capable of choosing specific message states from among a number of alternatives, none of which is either impossible or necessary. On the other hand, whenever a choice among alternative states is made and indicated by S, information is conveyed in that indication, since uncertainty regarding which state S might choose is removed by reception of that indication.

The case for the negative is now at hand. From the viewpoint of information theory, only agents capable of choice are capable of communication. And since it appears at first glance that machines are not capable of exercising choice, we seem led to the conclusion that machines are not capable of communication, either with people or with other machines.

5. Thus we encounter what appears to be a basic dilemma for information theory. Either (1) machines can communicate with people, in which case (contrary apparently to common sense) machines are capable of choice, or (2) machines are not capable of choice, in which case (contrary both to common sense and to a common application of information theory) machines cannot communicate with people or with other machines. The only tolerable way out for information theory is to insist, with (1), that machines are capable of choice after all.

In the following I want to show that our initial disinclination to admit that machines can make choices is an illegitimate by-product of our disinclination to admit that machines can make decisions. I shall then argue that machines intrinsically are no less capable of choice, in the sense distinguished from decision, than are human beings.

II

6. Let us begin by exploring the conceptual boundaries between choice and decision.

It may be admitted at the outset that there is a use of the verb 'choose' which is similar to the customary use of 'decide,' and to that of other verbs expressing the resolution of indecision. When someone says, in an expression of resolve, "I have decided to stay," he might perhaps have said as well "I have chosen to stay," "I determined to stand my ground," or "I have made up my mind not to leave." Contrary to what seems to be the opinion of most recent writers on the topic,[6] however, this use surely is not paradigmatic of 'choice.' There is a more common use of the term[7] in which there is as much difference between a choice and a decision as between a cake and a recipe. These claims can be argued best with examples.

Consider the following sequence of events, involving both a decision and a choice. Mrs. B has won a contest sponsored by her favorite garden shop, in which the prize is the winner's choice among all the flowering shrubs displayed on the floor. Upon entering the shop to collect her prize, Mrs. B walks directly to a Japanese quince in a far corner and carries it to the counter to be released. Granted that her action is not haphazard, it is clear that Mrs. B *decided* before entering the shop that she would claim this particular plant. What is not clear at the moment is when exactly we should say that this particular plant was *chosen*. Should we say (1) that the decision and the choice were indistinguishable, one and the same mental act, so that Mrs. B's intention upon entering the shop was to pick up a plant she had already chosen? Or should we say (2) that the actual choice was not accomplished until she undertook physically to claim the plant for her own, in which case the act of choice would be identical with the act by which her prior decision was fulfilled?

There is, of course, as already noted, a sense of 'choose' in which (1) appears plausible. If a friend were to stop Mrs. B before she entered the shop and ask, "Have you made up your mind?" the answer would be 'yes' if she had reached a decision by that time and 'no' otherwise. That is, we often speak of the act of decision as a matter of making up one's mind. And we also often speak of the act of decision as a matter of making a choice. There is a sense therefore in which 'Have you made a choice?' and 'Have you made a decision?' are two ways of asking the same question. In this sense it would be natural for Mrs. B to say, upon being questioned whether her mind is made up, that the Japanese quince is her choice. In making up her mind she has chosen that plant, and nothing remains but to indicate her choice.[8]

So choice is not always distinct or distinguishable from decision. But surely this use is not paradigmatic in any general sense. On the contrary, there are expressions of many different sorts in which 'choice' is used to indicate an act sharply distinguishable from any resolution of indecision. Imagine (2a) that Mrs. B, when asked if her mind has been made up, replies, "Yes, I'm going to choose the Japanese quince." Now this remark clearly indicates that the decision has been made but that the choice has not; here the decision necessarily precedes the choice. Imagine again (2b) that Mrs. B picks up a dogwood plant instead, mistaking it for a Japanese quince. Here Mrs. B has chosen one thing, contrary to her decision, in favor of another. It is even possible, moreover, (2c) to reach a decision with regard to a matter in which no choice is ever actually made. Miss A, for example, may decide early in life to marry only a handsome, intelligent, and personable millionaire, with the result that she never comes to the point of actually choosing a mate. Or a presidential candidate may decide early in his campaign to nominate a particular person as his secretary of state, but being defeated, fails to have the opportunity to choose this or any other person for the post. Similar illustrations could be added ad libitum. In cases of each of these sorts the act of choice could not possibly be assimilated to the act of decision: in (2a) the decision necessarily is prior to the choice; in (2b) the choice runs contrary to the decision; and in (2c) the choice relevant to the decision is never made. Such situations are common enough at least to justify the claim that the use of 'to choose' in the sense of 'to decide' is not paradigmatic of that term.

In the sense illustrated by these examples, 'choose' has roughly the same meaning as 'select.' In (2a) Mrs. B, having decided in advance, promptly selects the Japanese quince. In (2b) Mrs. B selects the wrong plant, thus thwarting her decision in favor of the quince. And neither Miss A nor the presidential candidate in (2c), for all their ambition, ever finds the occasion to select the one upon whom preferment would be visited. This is the sense of the term 'to choose' to be examined here. Let us now turn to some of the more apparent differences between decision and choice, conceived in this sense of the term.

7. A basic distinction between acts of decision and acts of choice is that a decision, even on matters touching the public interest, can be made entirely in private, whereas a choice, even of most private intent, requires an overt and hence public performance. The context specifies the sort of performance required.

In some contexts of choice the necessary performance consists of a bodily indication of preference. The traveler might choose his way at a fork in the road by saying (to a companion), "Let's go left," by pointing his finger, or merely by setting out in the chosen direction. He may *decide* to go left while sitting motionless on a stone. But unless the traveler moves, speaks, points, or in some other way overtly indicates a definite preference, we would say he has not yet *chosen* his way. Similarly Mrs. B might decide to choose the Japanese quince in thoughtful privacy, but actually makes her choice when the clerk has been explicitly informed of her preference. In this use of 'choose,' to choose requires an indication of choice. To decide, on the other hand, does not require, and often does not invite, an indication of decision.

There is a related point of interest. Since an act of choice involves overt behavior, it is obvious that a particular choice can be made only in circumstances which accommodate behavior of the particular sort it involves. There is a time and also a place for choice. Correspondingly, there are times and places where a particular choice cannot be enacted. A decision, on the other hand, can be reached at any time and any place in which the agent has the presence of mind to achieve it. For example, Mrs. B can decide upon entering the contest, or some time thereafter, that should she win, the Japanese quince would be her choice; but the prize can be actually chosen only when the contest is over and the management willing. Again, student Q may decide (or have decided for him) while still in grade school that he will attend Harvard instead of Yale. But to speak of choosing Harvard over Yale in these circumstances would be at best presumption and at worst nonsense. Even as a graduating senior, moreover, the student can choose Harvard over Yale only if he receives offers from both schools. If only Yale accepts his application, it's Yale or nothing, and we would say the student has no choice.[9] In yet another circumstance, Mrs. B might decide to eat at the restaurant one evening before her husband is aware there is such an issue to be faced. Since choice requires propitious circumstances, however, Mrs. B does not have the privilege of choosing her restaurant, or of choosing to eat out at all, until the opportunity of choice is offered by her prospective escort.

8. We have seen that choice, but not decision, (1) requires overt performance, and (2) is dependent for its accomplishment upon appropriate time and circumstances. This suggests a third distinction even more fundamental. The expression 'I choose' frequently is used in a performative sense. The expression 'I decide,' on the other hand, is seldom used in any sense whatever.

To make a choice, as noted, is often merely to express one's intentions or to announce one's preference. Thus the traveler might choose his path by saying something to his companion, and Mrs. B might choose her prize by saying something to the clerk. And one of the more common things to say in choosing a path or a plant is, 'I choose that way' or 'I choose that one.' If Mrs. B, acting as winner of the contest, points to a plant and says to a clerk, "I choose that one," for Mrs. B to utter those words is for Mrs. B actually to make her choice. In short, the act of saying 'I choose (so and so),' given appropriate circumstances, itself constitutes an act of choice. This is what is meant by saying that 'to choose' is a performative verb.[10] By contrast, as we shall see, to say 'I decide (so and so),' apart from being downright odd in any save very special circumstances, at best could be construed as the report of a decision. To say 'I decide (so and so)' does not in itself constitute an act of decision.

To say 'I choose' in appropriate circumstances is not the only thing one might say in making a choice, any more than to say 'I promise' is the only thing one might say in making a promise. A promise can be made by replying 'I do' to the solemn question 'Do you promise?' and a choice can be made by replying 'That one' or 'This' to the question 'Which do you choose' or 'Which is your choice?' And there are many other ways of choosing by speaking. Mrs. B could also have chosen the Japanese quince by appropriate use of 'I prefer,' 'I would like,' 'May I have,' or 'Let me take.' The point is merely that when someone in a position to make a choice utters the expression 'I choose,' along with an indication of a particular object, course of action, or state of affairs available for choice, his saying this constitutes, at least in part, his actual choice of that alternative.

We should note, however, that the performative use of 'to choose,' like that of most other performative verbs, is limited to the first person, present tense. 'I choose (so and so),' appropriately spoken, can affect the choice of so and so; but 'I will choose (so and so),' 'I chose (so and so),' or 'He (she or it) chooses (chose, will choose) (so and so)' normally could be taken merely as predictions or statements of fact. Saying 'I chose (so and so)' at best is true and at worst is false, and nothing more is accomplished in the saying than a statement so favored or so deprived. In particular, to say 'I chose (so and so),' no matter how wishfully said, when in fact something else was chosen, neither nullifies the choice of that other thing nor retroactively effects an alternative choice.

It is interesting to note, in contrast, that 'to decide' also is peculiarly oriented toward use in a particular tense, not in the present as with 'to choose,' but in the past. In reporting or discussing a decision, one says 'I decided,' 'I have decided,' or 'I should have decided'; but one seldom has occasion to say anything like 'I decide' or 'I will decide.' Now it is not impossible to find a context in which the expression 'I decide' might sensibly occur. An executive might report, diffidently, his habits of reaching decisions by saying "I decide matters like that only after consulting my advisory board." But for someone to say 'I decide to go home,' intending thereby to report a decision, is of grammatical interest only as an example of what not to say. And there is a similar oddity in any expression of the form 'I will decide (so and so).'[11] One might say, in conjecture, that one probably will decide on a certain course of action. But to say without qualification that one will decide on a certain course of action strongly suggests that one has decided already and that the future tense is not appropriate. Of course one may say, again by way of prediction, that another person will decide (so and so), and intend this as a statement about the future. The statement by Paul that Peter will decide to sue may be either true or false. But the oddity of 'to decide' in the present tense carries over even in the second and third person. An expression of the form 'He decides (so and so)' usually would be used only in recounting another person's policy of decision-making, or perhaps to echo, in the historical present, another's announcement of a decision ("John decides to pass. Who will raise?").

Thus both 'to choose' and 'to decide' have their grammatical peculiarities, but are all the more distinct therein. Whereas 'choose' commonly is used to effect the making of choices, but only in the first person, present tense, 'decide,' seldom used in the present tense at all, is commonly used in the past to report decisions already made.

9. One reason for our disinclination to grant that machines can exercise choice may be the unexamined thought that choice is essentially bound up with purpose and deliberation. Given the prevalent concept of machine, however, it seems reasonable to say that machines are both incapable of deliberation and empty of intent. I wish now to show, contrariwise, (1) that although decision is necessarily preceded by deliberation, choice may be indeliberate, and (2) that decision, but not choice, necessarily is followed by an act of intention.

A choice, of course, might be deliberate. "He deliberately chose the toy I wanted" might express the complaint of a child against her brother. But choices need not be deliberate. Thus the mother might reply, to assuage hurt feelings, that the offending choice was not deliberate after all, since the brother was not aware of his sister's desires. If, in fact, it were not possible to choose indeliberately, it would be uninformative to ascribe deliberation to a particular choice. But the information conveyed in saying of an act merely that it was one of choice is not the same as that conveyed in saying of the act that it was one of deliberate choice. Since the expression 'deliberate choice' is not pleonastic, 'indeliberate choice' is not conceptually self-defeating.

The case is otherwise with acts of decision. Thus the child who complains "Susie deliberately decided not to invite me," cannot properly be assuaged by being told that the offending decision after all was not deliberate. To suggest this would be nonsense, for one simply does not make a decision without previously deliberating the matter. Susie might accidentally have overlooked some of her friends in making up the guest list. But once a decision has been made regarding the inclusion or exclusion of a particular name, there is nothing accidental or indeliberate about it. To speak of a 'deliberate decision' *is* to speak pleonastically, and 'indeliberate decision' is a self-defeating expression. Thus to say of a particular decision that it is deliberate adds no further information to the assertion merely that this decision has been made.

Consider now what might be said regarding the intention of an agent involved in an act of decision or, respectively, in an act of choice. We would not say, of course, that a person intended that a certain course of action be followed and subsequently decided upon that course of action. Mrs. B, for instance, did not first intend to choose the Japanese quince and then decide upon that choice. If the intention is active, the decision has already been made. But neither would there be occasion ordinarily to say of Mrs. B both that she decided to choose the Japanese quince and that she subsequently intended to choose that plant. The reason here, however, is not that intention in a certain regard cannot follow a decision in that same regard, but rather that the intention must follow the decision.[12] Just as it is uninformative, because necessarily true, to say that one has deliberated prior to having decided, so it is uninformative to say that one intends to do something one has previously decided to do.[13]

But it is otherwise with acts of choice. Whereas a decision is followed, but may not be preceded, by an intention in the same regard, a choice may be preceded, but may not be followed, by an intention to do what the choice accomplishes. Or, to put the same thing another way, a decision may not, whereas a choice might be preceded by an intention in the relevant regard; and a decision must, whereas a choice must not, be followed by the relevant intention. A choice accomplishing x may not be followed by an intention that x be the case. This is not to deny, of course, that once having made a choice a person may entertain certain intentions regarding the object he has chosen. Once Mrs. B has chosen the Japanese quince, she may intend to plant it in the rockgarden, and once Q has chosen Harvard he may fully intend to earn his degree. The point, rather, is that once a particular state of affairs has been accomplished by the enactment of a choice, any intention the agent may have had to bring about that state of affairs is no longer active. It is apparent that one cannot in any proper sense intend to do what in fact has already been done.

A final observation is in order about the relationship between decision and choice, given their involvement with acts of intention. Since decisions are invariably followed by relevant intentions, and since intentions in a relevant regard often precede choices, it stands to reason that decisions often figure among grounds for choice. Mrs. B chose the Japanese quince because she had decided before the contest began that this was the plant she wanted. We would not say in any normal circumstance, on the other hand, that a particular decision has been reached on the basis of a choice in the same regard. When the choice is made, the occasion is past, not only for further intentions, but also for any further decision in that particular regard.

Choices (but not decisions) are enacted, whereas decisions (but not choices) are carried out.[14] And one common way of carrying out a decision is to enact the choice by which the state of affairs fulfilling the decision is brought about.

III

10. The suggestion that machines can exercise choice may now ring less dull in sensitive ears. Yet it will still be protested that choice, although overt, and possibly indeliberate and unintentional, nonetheless is essentially a voluntary act. This may be taken to claim (1) that the act of choice is not constrained and (2) that the act of choice is consciously undertaken. We are likely to feel, on the other hand, that machines [a] *are* constrained and [b] are *not* conscious. Thus any admission that machines can exercise choice still seems blocked by conceptual impediments.

I shall attempt now to remove these final impediments by showing (contrary to [a]) that machines are *not* constrained, in a sense at least which would render them incapable of choice, and (contrary to [b]) that the act of choice *can* be accomplished nonconsciously.

11. The concept of machine is less clear today, with our masers, lasers, and photon-emission propulsion units, than in the days of the steam engine. But we still tend to think of machines somewhat as follows. Machines, as it were, run like clockwork. Their essence is predictability. Knowing how a machine has performed in the past (if it has

not begun to wear out), we feel entirely confident in predicting how it will perform in the future. Machines, in a word, are constrained, in the sense that their performance is completely predictable. But given this feature of complete predictability, it follows that machines cannot exercise choice of the sort bound up with the origination of information. As we have seen, an act is a source of information only if it removes some prior uncertainty; and since there is no uncertainty to be removed by behavior which is completely predictable, the occurrence of such behavior conveys no information whatsoever.

The refutation of this is not a point of logic but a point of fact. Machines simply are not constrained in the sense of being completely predictable, and in some respects are even less constrained than human beings. In point of fact neither machines nor men are either completely constrained nor completely unconstrained, and the proof is the same for either. If a system is completely constrained, as we have seen, it is incapable of originating information. And if a system is totally lacking in constraint, its behavior is random, and no one state of the system is capable of removing uncertainty either about another state or about the system's external environment. The result again is that the system is incapable of originating information. But both men and machines are capable of originating information as a matter of fact, either with regard to their internal states or with regard to their environment. Parallel to the patient who monitors his own condition through discussion with his physician, there is the computer which monitors its own performance through oscilloscopes, digital counters, and other internal sensing devices. And parallel to the military scout who probes the frontier to gain information for his commander, there is the space probe which gleans and processes information for the scientists with whom it communicates on earth. On a more mundane level, scientists recently have begun to plan completely automated laboratories, among hopes for which is that they will supply more pertinent information in a given time period than could the corresponding conventional laboratory staffed with human technicians.[15] This would be nonsense, which it is not, if all machines were completely constrained in the sense of complete predictability discussed above.

12. It remains to be shown that machines are not incapable of choice merely on the grounds that they are incapable of consciousness. Given that machines are not capable of consciousness (a matter not here open for debate), then indeed there is no lively issue whether machines are capable of decisions. Decisions involve both deliberation and intention, neither of which can be divorced from conscious behavior. Choice, on the other hand, being separable from deliberation and intention, is separable from conscious activity in general. Although a person might choose deliberately, me-

thodically, and in full awareness of the alternatives confronting him, he might also choose habitually or inadvertently, in either of which cases he might be unconscious of having made a choice. When Mrs. B selects the dogwood for her prize, mistaking it for the Japanese quince, she is not aware of having chosen the dogwood. And when someone votes a straight party ticket, he may choose a candidate for county coroner without being aware even that this particular candidate is running for office. From this it seems a short step to choosing a candidate without being aware that a choice is being made. The novice operator of the voting machine, for example, who pulls the lever prematurely and unmindful of the consequences has cast his vote regardless. It does not seem obviously incorrect here to say that this person actually has chosen his candidate before he realizes that the choice has been made.

We speak also of animals exhibiting preferences and making choices, without committing ourselves thereby on the question whether animals are conscious. Since cats prefer fish to vegetables, a cat will choose a catfish over a carrot each time the choice is offered. And although pigeons have no natural preference for squares over circles, they can be trained to choose one over the other in expectation of reward. At least we feel easy in talking this way, feeling at the same time a certain reserve about saying that the animal is conscious of what he is doing. Even if there were some sense in which we would be inclined to say the pigeon was conscious, surely it would sound more plausible to say he was conscious of the reward he anticipated than to say he was conscious of making a choice as such. Choice can be made a matter of habituation, and one thing about habitual action is that the agent often is not conscious in his performance of it. One person habitually chooses scotch, another reaches for a martini without thinking, but each makes a choice despite the indeliberate character of his act. So, too, we teach a child to select the smallest piece of cake offered, hoping that this choice will become habitual in his developed social behavior.

Consider, finally, the child who is offered his choice at the toy counter and impetuously picks up a toy car, which his father then purchases for him, only to insist later that he really wanted a toy gun. It will be useless for the child to protest, against his father's insistence that the choice has already been made, that he was not aware he could have the car *or* something else. Although the child may not have been aware that he had a choice, he has made a choice nonetheless, and perhaps in addition he has learned something about the grammar of the verb 'to choose.'

Although choice is often, and perhaps most frequently, a conscious activity, there is nothing in the grammar of the term which prohibits our saying that not all choices are consciously performed. No more than this is required for the present argument.

13. If my argument has been correct, there is

nothing amiss in speaking of choice-making by machine. Although it may be that the expression 'mechanical choice' has an odd ring about it, this merely reflects the fact that machines which invite this way of speaking have only begun to take their place in public awareness.[16] Regarding the mechanics of the matter, choice by machine is of a piece with natural selection, and reference to the latter is no longer awkward in public speech.

14. It is one thing to show that the concept of mechanical choice is not self-defeating, and quite another to analyze exhaustively the conditions under which we would say that a machine in fact has made a choice. I have attempted the former, insofar as I can anticipate contrary arguments worthy of a serious response. I have not attempted the latter. My guess in this direction, however, would be as follows. When (1) a distinction can be made between the machine and its environment, when (2) the machine responds to its environment by pursuing one among alternative courses of action not necessitated by its internal structure, and when (3) another agent, whether man or machine, is informed of features of the machine's environment by having been informed of the course of action it pursued, then I should say we are justified in speaking of the machine as having made a choice in the fullest sense of the term.

NOTES

1. Norbert Wiener, *The Human Use of Human Beings: Cybernetics and Society* (New York: Doubleday & Co., Inc., 1954), p. 16.

2. Another term often used is 'communication theory' or, in a wider application championed by Wiener, 'cybernetics.'

3. Some writers use terms other than 'choice' in reference to this act ('selection' or 'indication'). It is clear, at any rate, that if there is no range of alternative message states out of which the sender can form a unique representation of a given message, there is no possibility of communication.

4. The derivation of the formula and some of its basic applications are described in Chapter 11 of K. M. Sayre, *Recognition: A Study in the Philosophy of Artificial Intelligence* (Notre Dame: University of Notre Dame Press, 1965).

5. Choice of yes, when that choice is 50 per cent probable, conveys 1 bit of information; choice of a message state which is 25 per cent probable conveys 2 bits of information; and choice of a state initially 75 per cent probable conveys roughly 0.4 of a bit of information.

6. See J. L. Evans, "Choice," *The Philosophical Quarterly*, 5, 21 (1955), 301; W. D. Glasgow, "On Choosing," *Analysis*, 17, (1956–57), 139; T. F. Daveney, "Choosing," *Mind*, LXXIII (October 1964), 522; K. T. Gallagher, "On Choosing to Choose," *Mind*, LXXIII (October 1964), 481, 484.

7. In "Choosing, Deciding and Doing," *Analysis*, 18 (1957–58), 64, P. H. Nowell-Smith suggests, moreover,

on the authority of the *Oxford English Dictionary,* that this is the *root sense* of the term.

8. It is not the case, as seems to be suggested by Evans (*loc. cit.,* pp. 306 ff), that 'to choose' in its use synonymous with 'to decide' regularly takes an infinitive form as object. 'I do not choose to run' and 'He chose to take the Fifth Amendment' are intelligible, indeed, as announcements of decisions. But so also are 'He chose retirement' and 'He chose political martyrdom in the cause of civil liberty.'

9. Hobson's choice is no choice at all.

10. The best available account of performative utterances is still Austin's: see "Performative Utterances" in *Philosophical Papers,* J. O. Urmson and G. J. Warnock, eds. (Oxford, at the Clarendon Press, 1961); or better, *How to do Things with Words,* J. O. Urmson, ed. (Cambridge, Mass.: Harvard University Press, 1962). Also of interest is D. D. Evans, *The Logic of Self-Involvement* (London: SCM Press, 1963).

11. The point regards 'decide on,' 'decide that,' and 'decide to,' not 'decide whether' or 'decide what.' Expressions such as 'I will decide what to do tomorrow,' for example, are both common and proper.

12. A decision and an intention are "in the same regard" if the same expression (for example, 'to vote for X') when fitted into the blank of 'I decided . . . .' completes an expression of the decision and when fitted into the blank of 'I intend . . . .' completes an expression of the intention.

13. One may, of course, for special effect, emphasize what is obviously the case by saying, for example, both that he has decided and that he intends to go to Harvard. This might be one way of escaping duress from a father intent upon Yale. A common way of empha-

sizing what one has said is to say it again.

14. Legal decisions, not here in point, are both enacted and carried out.

15. See Daniel Cooper, "The Automated Laboratory," *International Science and Technology*, 36 (December 1964), 20–29.

16. Perhaps it is not really so odd after all. Henry Veatch remarks that a common misconception of the Aristotelian notion of moral virtue seems to stem from "the use of such expressions as 'learned habits of choice' or 'patterns of behavior' " which "suggest to us choices and actions that are habitual in the sense of being mechanical and unthinking." See *Rational Man: A Modern Interpretation of Aristotelian Ethics* (Bloomington: Indiana University Press, 1962), p. 110.

INFORMATION THEORY AND PHENOMENOLOGY

F. J. Crosson

... the whole question is ultimately one of understanding what, in the world and in ourselves, is the relation between meaning and absence of meaning.

                      Maurice Merleau-Ponty

IT DOES NOT TAKE MUCH READING IN CONtemporary philosophy to realize that the problem of meaning is central to our age. It is a logically primitive notion and an all encompassing theme for both conceptual and phenomenological analysis. At the same time, it is the subject on which they divide most sharply, the former stressing linguistic use as the matrix of meaning, the latter stressing preconceptual or prepredicative experience as the ultimate matrix in which meaning arises. The cold war which existed between these two methods of analysis during the 1950's is thawing, but as yet without much sign of fruitful exchange.

Part of the reason for this, I believe, is the lack of a conceptually useful sense of what is nonmeaningful, a sense which could be contrasted with what is meaningful in an illuminating way. Conceptual analysts have tended to rely on the rules of proper linguistic use to determine the limits of meaningful expressions and hence to define the matrix of meaning. One cannot go back beyond language use.

Phenomenological analysts while accepting the syntactic and semantic specifications of the nonmeaningful[1] make a distinction between sense and signification (*Sinn* and *Bedeutung*, *sens* and *signification*[2]) which points to a prepredicative level of meaning in perception. Conversely a perceptual kind of meaninglessness is exemplified, for example, in Husserl's thought-experiment of the destruction of the world.[3] In the case of perception the meaningful is related to the continuous fulfillment of expectations and is opposed therefore (by Husserl) to heterogeneous discontinuity or (by Merleau-Ponty) to complete homogeneity.[4] It is remarkable that both heterogeneity and homogeneity should fall under the nonmeaningful, and some possible reasons for this will appear later.

There are striking parallels between the phenomenological account of the structure of perception and some analyses in a field which might seem to be unrelated, information theory. The aim of this essay, however, is not merely to draw attention to such parallelisms. It is to suggest that information-theoretic analysis possesses a conceptually interesting counterpart to meaning and also provides a formal model for the analysis of perception.[5]

I

Information theory, following some earlier anticipations by Hartley (1928),[6] was brought to birth by Claude Shannon's work *The Mathematical Theory of Communication* in 1948.[7] Shannon's concern was to determine in some way the relation between the channel capacity of a communication system and the reliable transmission of messages through the channel. An intuitive, rough-and-ready measure of this might be to ask whether the receiver understood what the sender meant, what the latter wanted to convey by the message. But this measure could of course involve factors other than the message itself, for example, if the receiver was an intimate of the sender, mere hints and truncated allusions could be supplemented by personal knowledge. Moreover, Shannon was interested primarily in the technical dimensions of the message system, not in the meaning of the symbols transmitted (or more precisely the symbol-events). He needed, then, some unit of measure in terms of which to evaluate the quantity of the message, so to speak, and also the capacity of the channel.

Following the suggestions of Hartley, he proposed as a measure of the information given by each symbol the amount of uncertainty about what was going to be transmitted which the choice of this particular symbol resolves. The amount of uncertainty removed is of course a function of the probability (or improbability, a layman might add) of the occurrence of this particular symbol in comparison with others which might have been chosen. If an unlikely symbol is received, it conveys more information than one which was highly probable.

The sense of the term 'information' here, although not novel, is *not* the sense in which it is sometimes used as following on meaning. This has been a source of confusion by some writers who have glided from the nonsemantical use of the term by Shannon to the common use. In information theory, 'information' refers to the probability or uncertainty of a symbol or set of symbols and not to its meaning. This use is not without precedent in ordinary language. Suppose a brief recorded sentence is played over and over again. After the first few hearings, although it remains meaningful, it ceases to convey any information. Its reiteration is without any surprises, it "tells us nothing new," it removes no uncertainty. Its probability is close to 1, that is, maximal.

If information, then, is measured in terms of the uncertainty which the message-events remove, it still remains to choose a unit of measure. This was arbitrarily but conveniently defined by Shannon as the logarithm to the base 2 of the number of possible message choices. In effect this means that the unit of information is the amount conveyed by a message which is one of only two equally possible messages, for example 1 or 0, yes or no. Such a message is defined to convey 1 bit (contraction of 'binary digit') of information. If we are playing "Twenty Questions" and I ask "is it mineral?" the response will convey 1 bit of information to me since only two answers are possible and by supposition here equally probable. If I ask, "Is it mineral, vegetable, animal or human?", assuming it is one of these, the answer will yield 2 bits of information, since $4 = 2^2$ and hence $\log_2 4 = 2$. If I name eight categories in the question all of which are equally probable, the answer will yield 3 bits of information ($\log_2 8 = 3$), and so on. Whenever the number of equiprobable message choices is reduced by one-half, 1 bit of information is conveyed.

We can express this in a formula. Let $I(s)$ represent the information per symbol s. Then $I(s) = \log_2$ of the number of possible choices. For the last example above, $I(s) = \log_2 8 = 3$ bits. Now let S = the set of possible choices for the message. If they are all equally probable, then the probability of each one will be simply the inverse of the total number. If there are two choices (yes or no), the probability of each is $\frac{1}{2}$. If there are four possible choices, the probability of each is $\frac{1}{4}$. In general, if P(s) stands for the probability of some one symbol, then

$$I(s) = \log_2 \frac{1}{P(s)}$$

or in a mathematically equivalent form,

$$I(s) = -\log_2 P(s)$$

So far we have been considering only single symbols and their information. But a message may consist of a number of symbols selected from the source alphabet. Let $s_i, s_j \ldots$ stand for the successive symbols of the message, selected from the source-alphabet $S = \{s_1, s_2, \ldots, s_n\}$, each having a fixed, independent probability of occurrence. Then the total information of any particular message will be the sum of the information content of all its component symbols. The likelihood of our receiving any particular amount of information $I(s_i)$ is $P(s_i) I(s_i)$. This means that if we ask what in general will be the average amount of information per symbol from this source, the answer is the sum of those particular probabilities:

$$\sum_S P(s_i) I(s_i)$$

This quantity is the nucleus of information theory and is called the entropy of the source or the average amount of information per symbol and is symbolized by the letter H. This symbol and the term 'entropy' are borrowed from statistical thermodynamics, where a similar formula occurs:

$$H(S) = \sum_S P(s_i) I(s_i) = \sum_S P(s_i) \log_2 \frac{1}{P(s_i)} \text{ bits}$$

If all the symbols of the source alphabet are equally probable, H(S) will of course simply be the probability of any one symbol. If they are not equally probable, H(S) will be the statistically average amount of information.

Take, as the simplest example, flipping a coin. Then S = {heads, tails} and since these are equiprobable, the probability of each is the inverse of the total number: ½. Hence

$$I(s_1) = \log_2 \frac{1}{P(s_1)} = \log_2 2 = 1 \text{ bit}$$

and the average amount of information per flip (message)

$$H(S) = \sum_S P(s_i) \log_2 \frac{1}{P(s_i)} = (½ \times 1) + (½ \times 1) = 1 \text{ bit}$$

Message sources such as we have been discussing, where the probabilities of each symbol are independent and fixed, are called zero-memory sources. As such they are instances of what are called "stochastic processes." A stochastic process is a

> system which produces a sequence of symbols (which may of course be letters or musical notes,

say, rather than words) according to certain probabilities.[8]

But by far the most interesting and useful class of stochastic processes are systems in which the probabilities of the symbols produced are not fixed and independent but rather are a function of the previously produced or emitted symbols. Such stochastic processes are called Markoff processes or Markoff chains, after the Russian mathematician who first investigated them.[9]

In a Markoff process, the probability of the occurrence of a particular symbol s_i is a function of the preceding m symbols, and the system is called an m-th order Markoff source. The conditional probability of s_i is expressed as

$$P(s_i/s_{j_1}, s_{j_2}, \ldots, s_{j_m})$$

and the symbols $s_{j_1}, s_{j_2}, \ldots, s_{j_m}$ which determine the probability of s_i are called the state of the system. Given this expression, the earlier equations for $I(s)$ and $H(S)$ can easily be written for a Markoff source by simple substitution.

It is clear that a Markoff source will have constraints on the choice of successive message symbols on the basis of the state of the system, that is, the symbols previously emitted, and that consequently the average amount of information per symbol will decrease. The latter phrase simply means there will be less uncertainty that (greater probability that) a particular symbol will be emitted when the system is in a given post-initial state. This can be put intuitively in psychological terms by saying that the receiver will anticipate s_i, will be less surprised by its occurrence, and so will be less informed by it.

A simple example of this is provided by the sequence of letters in a page of ordinary prose. The occurrences in such a context of the different letters of the English alphabet are not equiprobable. Consequently the maximum possible entropy (average uncertainty) of a sequence of letters which would be realized only if they were all equiprobable is decreased by the constraints of the conventional rules of spelling, so that the actual entropy is substantially less. In the case of a particular source alphabet, say the actual entropy may be 70 per cent of the maximum entropy, and in this case the redundancy of the source alphabet is 30 per cent.

The redundancy is

> the fraction of the structure of the message which is determined not by the free choice of the sender, but rather by the accepted statistical rules governing the use of the symbols in question.[10]

As before, when entropy was defined as the average uncertainty per message symbol of an indefinitely large set of messages from a specific source, so here redundancy refers not to a particular message but to the characteristic of any message in a specific source alphabet. 'Redundancy' as thus defined is unlike one of its common senses, that by which we refer to the redundancy of a particular sentence in virtue of a superfluity of synonyms.

With these essentials of information theory at hand, we are in a position to see the fruitfulness of its application to simple and unchanging, and to complex and changing instances of perception.

II

A small but significant amount of work by experimental psychologists has shown the utility of information-theoretic methods in the analysis of the perception of static figures. Perhaps the most exciting result has been the explanation of the "Gestalt qualities," such as "figural goodness" in these terms. The importance of this work lies in the fact that qualitative characteristics such as the one mentioned have been shown to be amenable to formal analysis. Specifically the experiments demonstrate that the Gestalt qualities constitute redundancy in visual stimulation and so may be expressed quantitatively.[11] But they do more than provide a measurement scale for such patterns. They also pose and verify the hypothesis that the tendency of the organism is to perceive in terms of figures of maximum internal redundancy.[12] Such a figure, as we have seen, will possess less information, or to put it another way, it is adequately specified by a proper subset of its parts. The Gestalt quality of "closure" is obviously related to this.

These last remarks raise a number of problems.

First of all, we have been talking about a particular set of inputs (the perceptual figure quantified, for example, by a superimposed grid), whereas as we noted above, information theory deals primarily with indefinitely large sets of messages to which probability functions can be applied and for which average uncertainty can be calculated. Thus Attnaeve speaks of the internal redundancy of a figure. Second, and related to this, we have implicitly been referring to nonconventional grounds of redundancy in citing Gestalt figures. For one of the insistent claims of the Gestalt psychologists has been that the unity of certain figures is to be explained by the "coherence" of their parts. This coherence is accounted for by the Gestalt qualities of good form, closure, good continuation, and so forth, and *not* by learning to see the figures as wholes, that is, by familiarity or convention. Hence it would appear that the redundancy of such figures is not based on the statistical probabilities of their "source-alphabet," at least in any plain sense.[13] We could summarize these objections as (1) that the use of the term 'redundancy' in this context seems to be based not on statistical constraints on the elements of a message, but on a consequence of this, namely the possibility of restoring the whole when some of the parts are lost, and (2) that there seems to be no conventional source-alphabet whose conditional probabilities would account for redundancy.

It is true that conceiving of perception in terms

of a message is an extension of the original theory of communication. The question is whether this is a limping metaphor or whether it is a workable model.

If we think of the Gestalt qualities as constituting the source-alphabet of "good Gestalts," then both of the above difficulties seem to be mitigated if not dissolved. Although as yet we can only describe it as a "natural" alphabet, since it is just a fact that percipient organisms do tend to perceive in terms of these factors, it may well be that we will find another level of explanation for why these factors function as they do by considering the nervous system of the organism as a data-processing system with limited informational capacity.[14]

But whatever be the ultimate theoretical justification of it, it is beyond question that the definition of the Gestalt qualities in terms of their information redundancy has not only the advantage of quantification of a hitherto qualitative characteristic, but has genuine explanatory power, for example, in accounting for why simplicity predominates over symmetry.[15]

III

It is much more apparent that the concept of a stochastic process is appropriate when we turn to perceptual experiences which involve a temporal Gestalt. Here again we will be thinking of the self-information of a process rather than the mutual information of two sets of variables, $[I(X; Y)]$.

This distinction raises a critical point for the latter development of this essay, and a digression to consider it will be helpful.

The question at issue is critical because it is the point at which information analysis becomes relevant for the philosopher's concern with meaning. The thesis which will be argued is that there is an inverse relation between information and meaning. This has already been hinted at in the preceding discussion of several examples. Some information theorists seem to feel that relating them inversely dissociates the ordinary sense of information too radically from that of meaning.[16]

Consider as an example the current attempts to understand learning in terms of probability models.[17] The right and wrong moves involved in trial and error maze-learning will have varying and interdependent probabilities as the sequence of moves is produced through time. Learning of this sort is then a stochastic process, and the probability of a continuous sequence of correct moves will approach certainty as the time is extended and the number of trials increased (the particular time varying with different species and different individuals), if the subject is capable of learning the task. The stochastic process will then have a decreasing information content. If, on the other hand, the subject is not capable of learning the task, the sequence of right and wrong moves will vary more or less randomly; they will be tantamount to a series of equally probable guesses (depending on the complexity of the task). In this case the information content of the series of trial runs will remain high.

The two uses of the term 'information' in the last paragraph both refer to self-information: the average information content of an ensemble of trial runs through the maze, each consisting of a sequence of right and/or wrong moves. Let $H(X)$ represent this content for the "stupid" subject (who cannot learn the maze) and $H(Y)$ represent this content for the "intelligent" subject. Then as noted $H(X)$, the entropy of the series of stupid trials, will be significantly high relative to $H(Y)$, the entropy of the intelligent trials, which will tend toward zero as learning progresses.

The mutual information of any two ensembles, $I(X; Y)$,[18] will have a positive value unless their elements are statistically independent. To take a usual example, if the X ensemble is the set of inputs into a communication channel and the Y ensemble is the set of outputs, then the mutual information will be the amount of information which they share. For a perfectly noiseless channel and no ambiguity in coding, the mutual information will be maximal. As noise and equivocation increase, there will be less correlation between input and output ensembles, and the mutual information will decrease.

Now suppose we observe a decerebrated animal which is incapable of learning the maze into which it is placed. We could say that its behavior is meaningless, that there is no increase in the likelihood of correct turns; this entails that there will no correlation between its performance and that of a successful learner: $I(X; Y) = 0$. One of the reasons why we call it meaningless is indeed its random character, and this implies its high self-information content and its low or nil mutual information. Information about the sequence of moves of a learner tells us nothing about the sequence of moves of our stupid animal, and vice versa. From this point of view, meaning is related to mutual information rather than to self-information.

This view of meaning intuitively fits not only ordinary uses of the term, but also definitions of the term by philosophers. Most such definitions or analyses agree in locating meaning in a triadic relationship in which one of the relata is significant with respect to another relatum for some subject. For example, M. R. Cohen:

> ... anything acquires meaning if it is connected with, or indicates, or refers to, something beyond itself, so that its full nature points to and is revealed in that connection.[19]

And similarly, M. Merleau-Ponty:

> That a quality, an area of red should signify something ... means ... that it announces something else which it does not include. ...[20]

But to say that meaning involves something pointing beyond itself is ambiguous. For what is pointed to may be another or other elements in the process or whole of which the meaningful element is a part, or it may be something outside and different from that element or whole. The importance of distinguishing these cannot be overemphasized. We shall, following Merleau-Ponty, call the first of these "sense" and the second "significance." The events of a process, then, can have sense (or "make sense," as we generally say in English) or have significance if they "point beyond," and they will have one or the other depending on what they "point" to.[21]

Recall that information is directly related to the degree of freedom of choice by which symbols are selected from a source alphabet. If anything at all may occur next, the information is high: we "don't know what to expect." But every limitation imposed on the selectivity results in a decrease in the quantity of information which the selected symbols contain. As the average uncertainty or entropy of the symbols decreases, redundancy increases, and the sequence (or sequences) begins to "make sense." We are oscillating here between technical and psychological descriptions of the process in order to make plausible the correlation of these which we are trying to establish.

This interpretation can be illustrated by turning to an example which the Gestaltists constantly used as an instance of a temporal configuration and which has received more information analysis than any other art form—music.[22] Here again earlier qualitative analysis has yielded in part to formal and quantitative analysis and has made possible mechanical composition of music.

Meyer argues that music is a Markoff process, and that if this is so,

> it would appear that as a musical event (be it a phrase, a theme, or a whole work) unfolds and the probability of a particular conclusion increases, uncertainty, information and meaning will necessarily decrease.[23]

This last line suggests a direct rather than an inverse relationship between meaning and information, but I think that this is unsatisfactory, even for his own analysis. I shall return to this shortly.

In Meyer's view, the constraints which limit the possible randomness of the elements of the musical process (tones, timbre, silence, loudness, and so forth) are the transition probabilities which characterize musical styles, and we may add, specific composers.[24] His definition of meaning is:

> Musical meaning arises when an antecedent situation, requiring an estimate as to the probable modes of pattern continuation, produces uncertainty as to the temporal nature of the expected consequent.[25]

But this is an evaluative not a descriptive definition of meaning, because it implicitly requires that not just any uncertainty be produced. An indication of this is his comment on modern music, which because of its random character is difficult to follow:

> ... in their zeal to "pack" music full of meaning some contemporary composers have perhaps so overloaded the channel-capacity of the audience that one meaning obscures another in the ensuing overflow.[26]

Surely it is clear, as even the technical term 'channel-capacity' suggests, that it is information with which the music is overloaded, and that this is precisely why it doesn't "make sense," that is, have meaning.

A counter-witness to Meyer's thesis about the relation between meaning and information (which, it may be added, does not detract from the validity and insight of his analysis of meaning in music) is to be found in a review article by E. H. Gombrich of a book by M. Peckham, *Man's Rage for Chaos*.[27] The book and the article are innocent of any reference to information theory, but they perfectly exemplify the material in the arts for such analysis.

Peckham's contention is that the function of the artist is to produce a shock of surprise: "his role requires him to create unpredicted situations." Gombrich summarizes the book's central thesis: "the work of art comes into being by what [Peckham] calls 'discontinuity,' the violation of form or more exactly of the receiver's expectation." This is, the reviewer responds, a half-truth: if a deviation from the expected were the only requirement, any false note would do the trick. Great art does indeed arouse expectancies which are not fulfilled in a familiar, trite way, but they are fulfilled: "we find to our delight that the master knows of a better, more unexpected and yet more convincing way to take us home to the tonic on an adventurous road."

It is not, then, the unexpected, the random as such which is directly related to meaning in the arts. If it were, it would be hard to understand why we return again and again to great works. The point which generates confusion is that part of the delight in aesthetic appreciation is due to the interplay of information and meaning. Specifically, 'interplay' here refers to the retroactive or retrospective assimilation of what seemed unpredictable to the developing sense of the process. We see that we could (and perhaps should) have anticipated the unexpected event. It is the converse of the conditional probabilities of the stochastic process referred to earlier[28] which come into play here, and the restrospectively recognized redundancy confirms the meaningfulness of the unexpected event. The exception tests the rule, and once again we arrive at the conclusion that redundancy, low information, and meaning go together.

IV

The basic outlines of the argument of this essay are now in view. It remains to expand the argument by applying it more broadly and to develop some of its ramifications. This will be done by utilizing it for an analysis of the phenomenological theory of perception and then using it to interpret the notion of meaning in Husserl and Merleau-Ponty.

We may begin by quoting from an American philosopher who has affinities with phenomenology, or at least common oppositions in this case, John Dewey.

> . . . in any object of primary experience there are always potentialities which are not explicit; any object that is overt is charged with possible consequences that are hidden; the most overt act has factors which are not explicit.[29]

A good deal turns on how descriptively we take these references to potentialities or implicit aspects of perceptual objects. Do we mean that the implicit factors are really given with the overt, or do we mean that memory or inference frames the overt with associations?

Both alternatives have been and are held for persuasive reasons by different philosophical traditions. The latter alternative has been cogently argued by David Hume, among many others, and the clarity of his analysis lends itself to the purpose of comparison.

Experience consists for Hume in the succession of perceptions (whether ideas or impressions) in the mind. The impressions, like the ideas, are naturally clustered into complex perceptions by relations of continuity, resemblance, and causality (or regular sequentiality). But these relations are factual and contingent: they happen to be the way in which perceptions have been related in the mind during past experience. We never discover any necessary relations between impressions of external objects. We only find that the one does actually in fact follow the other.

> All events seem entirely loose and separate. One event follows another; but we can never observe any tie between them. They seem conjoined, but never connected.[30]

Moreover what we call external objects are made up of many simple impressions which have no necessary relation to one another, for example, "a particular colour, taste and smell are qualities all united together in this apple." It follows that the order of impressions itself provides no necessary nor even probable grounds that the future will be like the past: anything can happen. Snow falling from the sky may have "the taste of salt or feeling of fire." There is no "more intelligible proposition than to affirm that all the trees will flourish in December and January, and decay in May and June."[31]

There is a remarkably precise category in information theory with which to describe Hume's picture of perceptual experience, the concept of zero-memory. A zero-memory information source is one which emits a sequence of symbols which are statistically independent. There are no transition probabilities, so that we can never say on the basis of what has been emitted what is likely to follow, or more precisely, what has been emitted does not increase or decrease the probability of what will be emitted next. Consequently no redundancy is introduced into the sequence, and it ought not, on the basis of our earlier argument, to make sense. In itself, as Hume's argument shows, the sequence of impressions does not. We do believe constantly in a regular, external order of nature, but while this is understandable, it is not grounded in reason.

The belief in an external world and the correspondence of our experience with it can be expressed in terms of mutual information. If we think (as the empiricists did) of the senses as communication channels with the external world, then the order of events in the world will constitute the input and the order of our impressions will constitute the output of the channel. When we specify the probabilities $P(a_i)$ of the input alphabet A, the probabilities $P(b_j)$ of the output alphabet B, and the forward conditional probabilities $P(b_j/a_i)$ (the probability that b_j will be received when a_i is produced), then we have adequately described a zero-memory information channel.[32] Physiological psychologists constantly approximate the calculation involved in such a description of a particular channel when they establish empirical correlations between, for example, light wavelengths and the experience of colors. The mutual information $I(A; B)$ in such experimental instances is very high. Once the channel is described, we can calculate the backward probabilities $P(a_i/b_j)$, the probability that an input a_i has been produced when the output b_j has been received.

We cannot use the model of a channel for Hume's theory, however, despite his reference to the senses as "inlets," because in his view we have no independent access to the input data and their probabilities, and hence no conditional probabilities:

> The mind never has anything present to it but the perceptions, and cannot possibly reach any experience of their connection with objects. The supposition of such a connection . . . is, therefore, without any foundation in reasoning.[33]

It appears then that only the self-information model is appropriate here, and as it was indicated above, the "fit" of the model is good.

But one part of Hume's theory finds as yet no corresponding place in the model: our ungrounded belief in the external world, that is, in the continued regularity of the sequence of impressions. Since, however, this "making sense" of the impressions is psychological, due to relations among them which are introduced by the perceiver, it is clear that the zero-memory system is apt. What we need to supplement the latter is a separate source of transition probabilities which could make the process meaningful.

Such a supplement may be found in the formal characterization of meaning proposed by D. M. MacKay.[34] MacKay suggests that any event detected by an organism or machine may exercise a selective function on the transition probability matrices of the detector, matrices which determine the attitude or orientation of subsequent behavior. The meaning of the event is defined by the particular value of the selective function, that is, by the matrix which it activates in the organism.

There is ample physiological and behavioral evidence to indicate there are "different specific ways of processing incoming information: these different methods correspond to different ways of classifying incoming information. Probably part of what an animal faced with a discrimination task learns is to switch in the correct analysing mechanism. . . ."[35]

Such a characterization of meaning is of course "subjective," but this is exactly what a model of Hume's theory requires.[36] The stochastic process of the sequence of impressions makes sense, not by virtue of its intrinsic redundancy, but because of associative relations established by the percipient.

In definite contrast to this is the phenomenological analysis of perception, according to which every object of awareness has "potential" as well as "actual" aspects which are given (data) just as much as the actual aspects, though of course not in the same manner.

> . . . every actuality involves its potentialities, which are not empty possibilities, but rather possibilities intentionally predelineated in respect of content. . . .
>
> The predelineation itself, to be sure, is at all times imperfect; yet with its indeterminateness it has a determinate structure. For example: the die leaves open a great variety of things pertaining to the unseen faces; yet it is already "construed" in advance as a die, in particular as colored, rough, and the like, though each of these determinations always leaves further particulars open. This leaving open, prior to further determinings (which perhaps never take place) is a moment included in the given consciousness itself; it is precisely what makes up the [internal] "horizon."[37]

The aim of this analysis is to acknowledge both the determinate and limited character of perceptual data, and their determinable and referential character. A perception of a body from one side is a perception of a *body* from *one* side. As Husserl remarked, "the seen side is a side only insofar as it has unseen sides, which as such are anticipated in a determinate sense."[38] The internal horizon or system of implicit references to other aspects constitutes the perceptual *meaning* of what is explicitly given (the *Wahrnehmungssinn*).

The implicit nature of the references must be stressed as well as their given quality. It is a frequent mistake to suppose that the phenomenological claim is that "independently of any previous experience, an observer would be able to *infer* from the look of one side of the mountain that it had another side."[39] The determinate and the determinable are *both* modes of appearing,[40] both part of the data: the internal horizon is not an inferential construct, something added to the data.[41]

This point can be expressed in terms of the model developed for Hume's theory of perception by recalling that in that model the event perceived gives rise to meaning but does not possess meaning intrinsically. The impression-event is a sign, in the terminology of Charles Morris:

> S is a sign of D for I to the degree that I takes account of D in virtue of the presence of S.[42]

But this definition seems to require that the apprehension of D be distinct from the apprehension of S, or, in other words, that S be sign-ificant, be grasped, reflectively at least, as a sign.

Husserl always insisted that no such awareness accompanied perception.

> The spatial thing which we see is, despite all its transcendence, perceived, we are consciously aware of it as given in its embodied form. We are not given an image or a sign *in its place*. We must not substitute the consciousness of a sign or an image for a perception.[43]

It is the object itself which is presented to us in perception and not an effect or representation of it. But it presents itself as a real, physical object, as "transcendent" to our experience of it, precisely insofar as it does not yield itself fully, that is, insofar as it presents itself as having other aspects. Husserl writes, "each phase of perception [is] a mere side of 'the' object, as what was perceptually meant. This *intending-beyond-itself,* which is implicit in any consciousness, must be considered an essential moment of it."[44]

It is clear that for phenomenology perception is a Markoff process and hence one in which meaning must be defined in terms of the self-information of the process, or more precisely in terms of the redundancy introduced by the transition probabilities of the internal horizon. The references constituting the latter are probabilities in two precise senses: (1) as indicated above, the references are "at all times imperfect," that is, more or less determinate; and (2) the probability of the references, individually or collectively, never reaches certitude. Confutation of the predelineated aspects is always possible.[45]

A corollary of this view is that perception is an unmediated apprehension, so that the model of a communication channel does not seem to apply. It may be that Husserl's noetic-noematic correlation could be modeled in this way, but this would take us too far afield at present.

V

We turn now to the last of our topics, the exemplification of meaninglessness in two contrasting examples.

The first of these is Husserl's thought-experiment of the "nullifying" of the world. As we have seen, perception is for him an open-ended process. A thing presents itself as real to the extent to which its giveness includes indications for future perceptions, and those indications continue to be fulfilled by actual subsequent perceptions. If they are not fulfilled or if they are fulfilled in a wholly unexpected way, the meaning of the whole process of perceiving this object is transmuted: it becomes an illusion or a perception of a different object. "I thought I saw a man in the store window, but when I got closer I saw it was only a reflection." "I thought I saw a squirrel by the tree, but on closer examination it turned out to be a leaf."

Both these examples are of particular objects within a perceptual context which remains constant and real, that is, in which the anticipated aspects of the store front or of the tree (and their surroundings) continue to be fulfilled as we move toward them. The natural world as a whole remains real for us, according to Husserl, precisely inasmuch as the process of the coincidence of pre-delineated aspects and actual subsequent perceptions continues. "The existence of a world is the correlate of certain experience-patterns marked out by certain essential formations."[46] The existence of each real thing and of the world as "the totality of objects that can be known through experience"[47] is thus presumptive or contingent in the sense that no complete fulfillment of the system of implicit references is possible. The "reality-status" of any and every physical object is always subject to modification in the light of subsequent experiences.

Suppose now that in fact none of the "potential" aspects of current experience (aspects which, as we have seen, constitute the meaning of the perceptual object) were fulfilled from moment to moment. The world—the regular unrolling of ordered patterns—would exist no longer. We might not quite have a "blooming, buzzing confusion," because

> to a certain extent still, rough unitary formation might be constituted, fleeting concentration-centers for intuitions which were the mere analogues of thing-intuitions, being wholly incapable of constituting self-preserving "realities," unities that endure and "exist in themselves whether perceived or not perceived."[48]

Such a process would cease to make sense as the uncertainty about subsequent moments increased. Information-content would be maximal because it would be impossible to predict what would follow. Experience would be meaningless since "Reality and world . . . are just the titles for certain valid unities of meaning,"[49] namely, the Markoffian perceptual processes.

In contrast to this are Merleau-Ponty's remarks on the undifferentiated perceptual field. Following the Gestaltists, he affirms that the simplest possible sensible datum is a figure on a ground. Any such perceptual structure already has a sense: "Each part arouses the expectation of (*annonce*) more than it contains, and this elementary perception is therefore already charged with *meaning (un sens)*."[50] For example, in a light patch on a dark ground the patch stands out and does not interrupt the ground which appears to extend under it, and so forth.

If this is the simplest possible perception, then a "really homogeneous area offering nothing to perception cannot be given to any perception."[51] It is possible to establish such a perceptual field under experimental conditions where a subject's face is located inside a large hollow hemisphere whose smooth surface is evenly illuminated. In such a case the subject "perceives no surface at all"; there is "complete lack of perceptual differentiation."[52] One literally does not see any thing. In such an experience the information content is minimal. Nothing changes; there is nothing to explore visually; every moment is exactly like its predecessors. It does not, in Merleau-Ponty's terminology, have sense or meaning (*sens*) because it has no differentiation and hence no structure.

Now it is curious that meaningless experiences appear at each end, as it were, of the information spectrum, both its maximal and minimal points. In terms of its meaninglessness, maximal randomness in the visual field is hardly distinguishable from minimal randomness.[53] Information is thus a term of greater extension than meaning.

Within the set of experiences which can be called perceptions, however, the relation suggested above between information and meaning seems to hold. If this is the case, then the "simplest perception"—for example, a white circle on a dark ground—should be maximally meaningful, especially as persisting through time. It makes sense, produces no surprises, and requires a minimal amount of information to define its shape.

This is not to say, of course, that it will be maximally *interesting*; it will very likely indeed be boring, just because nothing new is happening. These are psychological evaluations, and until now psychological categories have been carefully distinguished from information categories. Just as in the case of 'information' it was necessary to distinguish various connotations of the term, so also is the case for 'meaning' and its cognates. There is a connotation according to which one might say that a lecture is meaningful if it touches us deeply or shows us something new. To say this, it would seem, is to say not only that it made sense but also that it had unexpected content which required some measure of careful attention to grasp.

It is this connotation which was touched on earlier in referring to meaning in the arts. One speaks ordinarily of meaning in the arts in an evaluative and not a descriptive sense. More precisely, 'meaning' in this use implies not merely making sense but making sense plus having appropriate novelty, making sense in a novel way. So long as this distinction is recognized, there is no contradiction in admitting that an experience may make sense and still be "meaningless," that is, boring or trite.

Let me conclude with some cautionary remarks. The preceding pages are tentative in that they represent a first attempt to think of philosophical analyses of perception in terms of information theory. I am of course saying not that meaning is "nothing but" redundancy in a stochastic process, but rather simply that it can be fruitfully (suggestively) modeled by such a process. Theories of perception may never be adequately expressed in terms of the mathematical theory of information, but the categories and concepts of that theory can be of great help in clarifying philosophical analyses of perception.

NOTES

1. E. Husserl, *Logische Untersuchungen,* vol. II (Halle: Niemeyer, 1928) sections 10–14, distinguishes *Widersinn* and *Unsinn.* See F. J. Crosson, "Formal Logic and Formal Ontology in Husserl's Phenomenology," *Notre Dame Journal of Formal Logic,* III, 4 (October 1962) 259–269.

2. See the discussion of this difference in E. Husserl, *Ideas,* W. R. B. Gibson, trans. (New York: Crowell-Collier, 1962), section 124, p. 319.

3. *Ibid.* section 49.

4. M. Merleau-Ponty, *Phenomenology of Perception,* C. Smith, trans. (New York: Humanities Press, 1962), p. 4.

5. This brief contrast of language analysis with phenomenology passes over another type of conceptual analysis, that which retains close relations with formal logic. But here too the locus of the analysis of meaning

is propositional. Two quotations illustrate this: (1) C. I. Lewis, "The Modes of Meaning," *Philosophy and Phenomenological Research,* 4 (1944), 236: "Still, it is doubtful that there are, or could be, any meanings which it is intrinsically impossible for words to express: it may well be that in discussing verbal meanings exclusively, we do not necessarily omit any kind of meanings, but merely limit our consideration to meanings as conveyed by a particular type of vehicle"; and less cautiously, (2) P. Marhenke, "The Criterion of Significance" in *Semantics and the Philosophy of Language,* L. Linsky, ed. (Urbana: University of Illinois Press, 1952), p. 159: "In the absence of a criterion of significance . . . we are forced . . . to take significance, with respect to simple sentences, e.g. atomic sentences, as a primitive notion. The decision whether or not a sentence not of this form is significant is made by a recursion procedure. For the simple sentences to which we are led by this procedure we have no test of significance."

6. R. V. Hartley, "Transmission of Information," *Bell System Technical Journal,* 7, 535–563.

7. W. Weaver, "Recent Contributions to the Mathematical Theory of Communication" in Shannon and Weaver, *The Mathematical Theory of Communication* (Urbana: University of Illinois Press, 1963), p. 102.

8. *Ibid.*

9. In what follows we shall be dealing exclusively with ergodic rather than nonergodic Markoff sources. An ergodic source is one which "if observed for a very long time, will (with probability, 1) emit a sequence of source symbols which is 'typical' ": N. Abramson, *Information Theory and Coding* (New York: McGraw-Hill, 1963), p. 23. See also W. Weaver, *art. cit.,* p. 102.

10. Weaver, *art. cit.*, p. 104.

11. F. Attnaeve, "Some Informational Aspects of Visual Perception," *Psychological Review*, 61 (1954), 183–193.

12. Attnaeve, *art. cit.* See also J. Hochberg and E. McAlister, "A Quantitative Approach to Figural Goodness," *Journal of Experimental Psychology*, 46:5 (1953), 361–364, where the thesis is formulated: "the probability of a given perceptual response to a stimulus is an inverse function of the amount of information required to define that pattern."

13. See the formulation of these criticisms in H. Quastler, *Information Theory in Psychology* (Glencoe, Illinois: Free Press, 1955), pp. 21, 300. For a general caveat on the application of information theory to psychology see the article of L. J. Cronbach, "On the Non-Rational Application of Information Measures in Psychology," *ibid.*, pp. 14–30.

14. See the essay of K. Sayre in this volume, "Toward a Quantitative Model of Pattern Formation."

15. F. Attnaeve, "Symmetry, Information and Memory for Patterns," *American Journal of Psychology*, 68 (1955), 209. Compare the variant results (for memory of words) and critical comments of G. Miller, "Human Memory and Storage of Information," *IRE Transactions of Informative Theory*, I T-2, 3 (1956), 129.

16. See the essay of J. Massey in this volume, "Information, Machines, and Men," p. 45.

17. R. Bush and F. Mosteller, *Stochastic Models for Learning* (New York: Wiley, 1955). For a brief survey and selected bibliography, see W. Sluckin, *Minds and Machines* (London: Penguin, 1960), pp. 157–187.

18. For a definition of this expression, see Abramson, *op. cit.*, p. 106.

19. M. R. Cohen, *A Preface to Logic* (New York: Henry Holt, 1944), p. 47, quoted in L. B. Meyer, "Meaning in Music and Information Theory," *Journal of Esthetics and Art Criticism*, XV, 4 (June 1957), 412–424.

20. M. Merleau-Ponty, *Phenomenology of Perception*, p. 13. See also *ibid.*, p. 428: "There is significance (*sens*) for us . . . when several terms exist *as* . . . representative or expressive of something other than themselves." The English translation, incidentally, hopelessly confuses the distinction referred to in note 2 above.

21. Meyer, *art. cit.*, distinguishes these as "designative" and "embodied" meaning and makes an illuminating application of them to music.

22. *Ibid.* Also L. Hiller and L. Isaacson, "Experimental Music" in *The Modeling of Mind*, K. Sayre and F. Crosson, eds. (Notre Dame: University of Notre Dame Press, 1963), pp. 43–71.

23. Meyer, *art. cit.* p. 419.

24. N. Hutler, unpublished paper.

25. Meyer, *art. cit.* p. 416.

26. *Ibid.* p. 420.

27. *New York Review of Books*, VI, 11 (June 23, 1966), 3–4.

28. See above, p. 105. In terms of information channels and mutual information (as distinguished from information sources and self-information) the probabilities referred to are called the forward and backward probabilities in reference to input and output. See Abramson, *op. cit.*, p. 99, and p. 101 on a priori and a posteriori entropy. These are relevant to the phenomenological theory of protentional and retentional aspects of experience.

29. John Dewey, *Experience and Nature,* Chap. I, quoted in *Intelligence in the Modern World,* J. Ratner, ed. (New York: Modern Library, 1939), p. 1043.

30. David Hume, *Enquiry Concerning the Human Understanding* (Oxford, at Clarendon Press, 1961), section VII, part I-II, pp. 63, 74. See *A Treatise of Human Nature* (Oxford, at Clarendon Press, 1960), p. 259: "... every distinct perception ... is a distinct existence, and is different, and distinguishable, and separable from every other perception, either contemporary or successive."

31. *Ibid.,* section IV, part II, p. 35. Hume is explicit about excluding probability as well as necessity: any argument which attempts to make past experience the standard for future experience "must be probable only .... But that there is no argument of this kind must appear if our explication ... be admitted as solid and satisfactory." *Ibid.* This is not to deny of course that we *do* proceed upon the supposition of future conformity, but merely to deny that we have any warrant for the supposition. See N. K. Smith, *The Philosophy of David Hume* (London: Macmillan, 1964), pp. 393 ff.

32. Abramson, *op. cit.,* p. 94 *et seq.* See these pages for a technical elaboration of this and the categories referred to subsequently.

33. Hume, *op. cit.,* section XII, part I, p. 153.

34. D. M. MacKay, "The Informational Analysis of Questions and Commands" in *Information Theory: 4th London Symposium,* C. Cherry, ed. (London: Butterworth and Co., Ltd., 1961).

35. N. Sutherland, "Stimulus - Analysing Mechanisms" in *The Modeling of Mind,* pp. 183–184. This article surveys present evidence for such mechanisms.

36. Our aim in this essay is not to adjudicate phil-

osophical differences, but to develop information-theoretic models for them. Meyer (*art. cit.,* p. 412) defends roughly the view mentioned here by saying, "while meaning is thus a mental fact, it is not arbitrarily subjective. The relationship between the stimulus and the thing to which it refers is a real relationship existing in the objective world. . . ."

37. E. Husserl, *Cartesian Meditations,* D. Cairus, trans. (The Hague: Nijhoff, 1960), pp. 44–45.

38. E. Husserl, *Erfahrung und Urteil* (Hamburg: Classen & Goverts, 1948), p. 31.

39. A. J. Ayer, "Phenomenology and Linguistic Analysis" in *Proceedings of the Aristotelian Society,* supplementary vol. XXXIII (1959), p. 117, emphasis mine.

40. This the title of a first-rate article which develops an analysis of perception in substantial agreement with that of phenomenology: C. M. Meyers, "The Determinate and Determinable Modes of Appearing," *Mind,* LXVII (1958), 32–49. The clearest exposition of the phenomenological description of perception known to me is A. Gurwitsch, *The Field of Consciousness* (Pittsburgh: Duquesne University Press, 1964), part IV.

41. No doubt the definiteness of the internal horizon is affected by past experience, but it seems clear that the organization and meaning of the sensory fields is not wholly the result of learning. After a review of experiments on perceptual processes in infants, D. E. Berlyne comments, "By this means, it has become evident that some degree of visual form discrimination, presumably innate, exists before learning has had time to mold perception, a question that was formerly open to debate." "Curiosity and Exploration," *Science,* 153 (July 1, 1966), 30.

42. C. W. Morris, "Foundations of the Theory of Signs," *International Encyclopedia of Unified Science,* vol. I, no. 2 (Chicago: University of Chicago Press, 1938), p. 4, quoted in Meyers, *art. cit.,* p. 41.

43. E. Husserl, *Ideas,* section 43, p. 123.

44. E. Husserl, *Cartesian Meditations,* section 20, p. 46.

45. E. Husserl, *Ideas,* sections 44 ff; *Phenomenology of Perception,* p. 297. There is, consequently, no certitude about particular physical things.

46. *Ibid.,* section 49, p. 136.

47. *Ibid.,* section 1, p. 46.

48. *Ibid.,* section 49, p. 137. Husserl's aim in describing this thought-experiment is to establish the dependence of the world on consciousness, but this is irrelevant to our purposes.

49. *Ibid.,* section 55, p. 153.

50. Merleau-Ponty, *Phenomenology of Perception,* p. 4.

51. *Ibid.* See K. Sayre, *Recognition: A Study in the Philosophy of Artificial Intelligence* (Notre Dame: University of Notre Dame Press, 1965), pp. 160–162.

52. D. Krech and R. Crutchfield, *Elements of Psychology* (New York: Knof, 1959), p. 85. The authors describe this as "the simplest possible percept." Whether it ought to be called a perceptual experience is a question. Aristotle says that we "see" that it is dark, and one might want to claim here, correspondingly, that we "see" (that it is) light.

53. Attnaeve, with his usual acuteness, has noticed this and commented in a similar vein. See his article referred to in note 10 above, p. 188.

TOWARD A QUANTITATIVE MODEL OF PATTERN FORMATION

K. M. Sayre

I

A PERCEPTUAL PATTERN IS WHAT A PERCIPIent makes of the parts. Pattern formation thus is a constituent of pattern recognition, whether in biological or in mechanical perceptual systems. That this is the case with human beings has been well taught by Gestalt psychology, and not forgotten in recent experimental studies of perception.[1]

The consequences for mechanical pattern-recognition, however, have been harder to assimilate. No analytic model exists by which the Gestalt relationships of part to whole and figure to ground can be rendered computable. The thought persists moreover that these relationships are insusceptible to quantitative treatment, and the alleged inability of digital computers to process the information involved in these relationships has been taken to establish an irresoluble difference between human and mechanical data-processing systems.[2] The task of mechanical pattern-recognition has thus been conceived as one merely of breaking data configurations into sets of salient features, the classification of which then amounts to the recognition of the original configuration.[3]

Yet the fact remains that any mechanical system capable of recognizing a data configuration as a pattern must be capable of responding to the configuration as a whole in a way not analyzable into a series of separate responses to discrete characteristics. Rather than argue in principle that this is possible, the aim here is to discuss one way in which such a system might possibly be accomplished.

The approach will be to provide a quantitative model in terms of which prominent features of pattern-responsive behavior in human beings can be analyzed and made computable. Insofar as the nervous system is conceived as a data-processing system, this model may serve as well as a tentative explanation of pattern formation in living perceptual systems. Among features of pattern perception treated are color constancy, double-aspect figures, pattern saturation, and the interaction between attention level and expectancy.

This model is based upon the concepts of self-information and of mutual information as defined in information theory. Let us begin by reviewing these concepts.

II

The self-information (or entropy) of an ensemble of events (X) is the amount of information needed on the average to specify an event in that ensemble.[4] Alternatively, the self-information of X is the upper limit of the amount of information the events of X can supply regarding events in another ensemble (Y). Since the information content of a single member (x_i) of X is expressible in terms of the probability of occurrence of x_i within X as follows:[5]

$$(1) \quad -\log P(x_i) ,$$

the information content of X is given in the equation

$$(2) \quad I(X) = \sum_X -P(x_i) \log P(x_i)$$

The intention of this study is to interpret analyzable patterns as ensembles of elements with information content measurable according to (2) and to treat unanalyzed patterns, or Gestalts, as elements with information content measurable according to (1). Although Gestalts are not themselves "mere" ensembles, they may be considered elements in ensembles either (i) of similar and related Gestalts through time or (ii) of dissimilar Gestalts within a percipient's field of awareness at a given moment. Thus considered, Gestalts can be assigned probability values reflecting their expected likelihoods of occurrence within a series of similar Gestalts or within a total perceptual field. Methods of assigning probability values with this effect are discussed below.

By "total perceptual field" is meant the totality of what perceptually appears to a percipient at a given moment. It will be assumed that distinct fields successively appear to a given percipient during succeeding moments in time, but no attempt will be made to formulate a general rule by which distinct fields could be delineated and numbered. Neither will an attempt be made to provide means for distinguishing and numbering specific Gestalts within a given perceptual field. I shall retain the liberty of speaking of faces, trees, animals, color configurations, and so forth alternatively as Gestalts or as ensembles of distinguishable elements, the use in point being indicated by context. For simplicity, discussion will be limited to the visual aspects of the total perceptual field, and no attempt will be made to relate the visual field to fields of other sense modalities.

When an undifferentiated event (v) is encountered within a perceptual field, the probability of occurrence of that event [$P(v)$] can be evaluated with reference to the expectancy of the observer. If v is an expected part of one's perceptual field (a chair appearing within one's view of his living room) at that moment, then $P(v)$ takes a value approaching unity. If v is the occasion for mild surprise (a cat in the chair when the cat was thought to be outside), then P(v) takes a middling to low value. And if v is a matter of considerable surprise, causes a start, or makes the observer look twice in disbelief, then P(v) takes a value approaching zero. One might perhaps be tempted to define P(v) in terms of the de facto frequency of appearance of a figure of a given sort within a particular type of visual context, but nothing would be gained in such an attempt, for the *measure* of P(v) must reduce ultimately to the degree of surprise or expectancy on the part of the observer encountering the figure v. We should bear in mind also that the expectancy reaction is built up by tutoring and extended learning experience, and it generally should not be expected to remain constant for any given figure from observer to observer. Certainly the expectancy of a single observer with respect to a given figure will not remain constant with varying perceptual circumstances. Apart from these considerations, moreover, any measure of expectancy would be meaningless beyond a certain comparatively low level of specificity. If sufficiently modest requirements (such as a ten point ranking system) are given, however, measures of expectancy are well within the reach of experimental techniques of contemporary behavioral science. If P(v) is given in quantitative terms, the self-information of v then is determined by formula (1) above.

The measure of self-information of an articulated figure is less direct but is along the same lines regarding expectancy or degree of surprise. Here we are concerned with the likelihood, or lack thereof, that a feature of a given sort will appear as part of the figure in question. If the appearance of a feature is common in a figure of a given type, $P(x_i)$ of that feature will be high; so, *mutatis mutandi,* for less common and highly uncommon features of the figure in question. In general any feature of a figure which varies from case to case among similar figures (as the presence of eyeglasses on a face) will have a probability less than unity (the value for invariant features) and greater than zero (the value for nonoccurrent features). The reason for a given probability level, however, is conceived here, not as a matter of frequency of actual occurrence of the feature within figures of the type in question, but rather a matter of the degree of expectancy or lack thereof associated with the appearance of that feature in the figure of a particular observer. Thus, for example, the appearance of a dominant white stripe along certain portions of a catlike form is less to be expected generally than the appearance of such a form without a stripe, catlike forms without the appearance of whiskers are generally expected to appear only under very special circumstances, and the appearance of catlike eyes in catlike faces is an expectancy with scarcely appreciable exception.

In some figures within some visual fields the distinct features which can be treated in terms of expectancy will be numerous. In other figures in other fields they will be few indeed. The limiting case is the undifferentiated Gestalt which appears quite literally as a whole without distinct parts. The number of distinct parts within a given figure is a variable which is dependent upon other features of an observer's on-going perceptual experience which we have yet to examine. For a given number (n) of such distinct parts (x_i), however, the self-information of their ensemble is simply

$$(3) \qquad -\sum_{i=1}^{n} P(x_i) \log P(x_i)$$

Thus, in general the greater the number of distinct elements x_i, the greater the self-information [$I(X)$] of the set X. Although the measure of $P(x_i)$ is in terms of expectancy, rather than of statistical frequency of occurrence within the set as in more common applications of information theory, the results are intuitively persuasive. In general, the more numerous the elements in terms of which communication is to be effected, the less anticipated on the average will be the occurrence of any given element; correspondingly, the more information is conveyed by the occurrence of a given element.

The experimental measurement of $P(x_i)$ for a given feature of a given configuration seems in principle to require little more ingenuity than the measurement of $I(v)$ for undifferentiated Gestalts.

It may be noted in passing that the degree of expectancy of an articulated pattern might also be obtained along lines suggested above when the pattern is considered as a unit. That is to say, it would be possible to obtain by independent measurements both $I(X)$ for a given articulated pattern (according to formula (2) and $I(v)$ for the same pattern without concern for its segmentation (by formula (1)). Thus, $I(X)$ might be determined for a face with pink cheeks, red nose, and green eyebrows; and another quantity $I(v)$ might be determined for the face as a whole without explicit regard for the idiosyncrasy of its parts. In this case $I(X)$ very likely will differ from $I(v)$ except in the limiting case where X is an ensemble of one. This is but another way of saying that the self-information value of a Gestalt is not equivalent to the sum of self-information values of its parts.

III

It is axiomatic in this discussion that the information-processing system of a conscious organism expends as little of its information-handling capacity upon a given perceptual task as is required by the current needs and interests of the organism.[6] As Attneave has insightfully remarked, "perception might be conceived as a set of preliminary 'data-reduction' operations, whereby sensory information is described, or encoded, in a form more economical than that in which it impinges on the receptors."[7] Our task for the remainder of this paper is to develop a model of these coding operations, particularly as they contribute to the formation of Gestalts within the agent's perceptual consciousness.

Consider the figure below, which might be taken either as an undifferentiated Gestalt or as a configuration of distinct parts.

(A)

The question How many parts?, however, fails to make sense without further specification of what counts as a part and of how one part is distinguished from another. In Attneave's words: "A visual stimulus array may not be said to contain any determinate number of *bits* of information until its grain—the size of its smallest elements—is specified."[8] What counts as a unit? If angles (or sides) are involved, there are three; if line segments of unspecified length, then the parts are of unspecified number. And if the parts are of unspecified number, the value of $I(X)$ for the triangle is unspecifiable.

There are of course various arbitrary ways in which the "grain" of the figure above might be specified. For example, one might impose the figure upon a square-celled matrix, or "grid," of arbitrary unit size. Now the point to note here is that the self-information content of a figure is in general a direct function (not a sole function) of the number of parts distinguished within it. And since the unit size of the grid is arbitrary, or at best a function of factors other than the figure itself, the self-information of the figure is arbitrary in the same sense.

For a simple illustration consider the imposition of the figure upon a 10 x 10 matrix as shown below. Consider further that the expectancy of occurrence of a triangle in the pertinent context has been established to be 5 per cent.

(B)

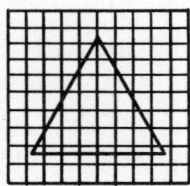

In the diagram as shown the triangle is divided into 21 parts. Thus, since the expectancy of occurrence of a part of the triangle is equal to the expectancy of occurrence of the triangle as a whole, $I(X)$ for the figure as shown may be calculated to be

$$-\sum_{i=1}^{21} P(x_i) \log P(x_i)$$

$$= -21 \times .05 \times \log .05$$

$$= -1.05 \times -4.32$$

$$= 4.54 \text{ bits of information}$$

If the figure is divided into only 15 parts as within the 6 x 6 matrix below, however, the assumption of a 5 per cent expectancy of occurrence of any one of its parts leads to the determination of a self-information content of 3.24 bits.

(C)

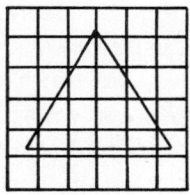

And, finally, if the figure is considered as having no distinct parts at all—that is, as an unanalyzed Gestalt—then the self-information content is merely 0.22 bits.

These simple reflections illustrate a way in which the perceptual information-processing system might be conceived to conserve its resources by handling configurations of data in terms of fewer rather than more articulated constituents. To reduce the self-information content of a set of data is to introduce redundancy within the set, which in turn is to form a pattern within an otherwise disparate collection of data. This creation of pattern, of course, is not analogous to the creation of forms in a block of marble by a sculptor. It is more nearly analogous to the way in which we create forms by sketching a tree in a few well-placed lines. In eliminating the large number of curved lines and angles that delineate the many leaves and branches in all their detail, we eliminate a great deal of information, but we retain overall enough information to deal effectively with the object in many practical contexts (for example, we can still identify it as a tree). The sense then in which the nervous system forms patterns may be conceived as a matter of cutting out needless information by decreasing the degree of articulation in which it processes a given set of data. The limit of this patterning process is reached when the configuration of data is treated as a unified symbol in itself—that is, as a Gestalt—without reference to any of the many elements which under other circumstances might be distinguished within it.

Such a tendency of the nervous system to reduce self-information content, it may be conjectured, is part of the mechanism behind the creation of Gestalts within the perceptual field. Through this process the percipient learns to treat familiar objects as wholes, devoting less attention (less information-handling capacity) overall to these than to unfamiliar objects, without appreciable sacrifice in his ability to deal with them effectively. To become thoroughly familiar with an object is to learn to react to that object as to a unified pattern, and for the nervous system accordingly to process information deriving from that object in a parsimonious fashion. Only when the appearance of a familiar pattern fails to integrate satisfactorily with the rest of his perceptual environment will the agent's information-processing system find it necessary to deal with the pattern as a configuration of discrete information-laden parts. The principles postulated as governing the level of articulation of a given pattern in these operations are discussed in section VI below.

We should pause at this point however to consider a basic objection to the suggestion that the nervous system patterns its incoming data in order to avoid undue information processing. At first thought this may indeed seem counterintuitive, for it is often said that what is familiar and highly patterned in our perceptual field provides *more* information about our environment than unfamiliar, loosely formed configurations. What is strange poses problems for the active organism, and what is familiar provides the information for solving them. But it is suggested above that the familiar pattern, as a Gestalt, contains *less* self-information than the unfamiliar. The resolution here is to realize that self-information is quite distinct from the sort of information provided about one's environment by the appearance of familiar (and redundant) figures in his perceptual field. This latter is what information theorists call "mutual information." Let us examine this second sense of 'information' in the context of other familiar Gestalt phenomena.

IV

Psychologists have documented the remarkable way in which colors appear to remain constant through changing conditions of illumination, and correspondingly the way in which objects retain apparently the same shape and size under varying conditions of perspective and distance. To the best of my knowledge however there is no satisfactory account of how the phenomena of color and shape constancy are grounded in the operations of the nervous system. In this section we shall consider a possible account of color constancy which can be rather easily transferred to shape and size constancy as well.

Now in a sense there are as many distinguishably different colors as there are distinguishable wavelengths in the so-called "visible range" of the electromagnetic spectrum. But we separate out only a few for specific notice, either to name them or to distinguish them explicitly within our normal perceptual fields. When colors vary only gradually from place to place, or from time to time, and our purpose (unlike the artist's) is merely to retain focus on the objects which the colors mark out in our perception, then we generally are not aware of whatever slight variations in color may occur. This is just another way of describing the phenomenon of color constancy. The reason we do not discriminate among subtly changing colors is that there is no call to do so, given our dominant interest of the moment, and that by not doing so we enable our nervous system to get by with less information-processing in this momentarily inessential regard.

To view the matter through information theory,

we need only consider that the self-information of a range of colors distinguished into 100 different shades is greater than the self-information of the range of colors less finely partitioned, say, into 50 different shades. This is the case regardless of whether the range of potentially distinguishable colors is spread within a single moment of perceptual awareness or is spread through time. The question of partitioning a series of shades spread through time, however, calls up the further question of the pragmatic purposes to be served in making any discrimination at all among various shades in the spectrum. If it is more economical in terms of information-processing to distinguish fewer different shades within the spectral range, why should not the nervous system merely treat all colors as one and respond instead (presumably as is the case with some lower organisms) merely to the presence or absence of illumination? The answer here is simply that the purpose of making color discriminations (and, to a point, of making any discriminations at all) is to allow the agent to anticipate successfully what is about to appear within his perceptual environment. Since color boundaries provide the basis for our distinguishing objects in our perceptual field, it is important to make rather fine color discriminations in order to retain a continuing focus upon a continually moving or changing object. The facts behind color-constancy phenomena, however, are that we require fine color discriminations less frequently than gross discriminations, and when gross discriminations enable us to maintain focus on objects of prime interest, we "systematically overlook" differences beyond the necessary degree of fineness. The mechanism which accomplishes this "systematic overlooking" is the information-processing system of the organism, and the principle according to which it is accomplished is that this system never expands more of its capacity on a given perceptual task than is necessary according to the current needs and interests of the agent.

It is time now to bring in from information theory an additional equation of basic importance. Whereas expressions (1) and (2) have to do primarily with the redundancy ("entropy") of a specific element or set of elements, this further equation has to do with the communication of information from a source to a receiver. Let us consider the ensemble X to comprise the elements in terms of which the message is received and the ensemble Y to comprise the elements in terms of which the message originally is conveyed. The receiver has X, as it were, within his total survey and knows or can determine all there is to be known about the number and distribution of its elements. The sender in turn knows all about the number and distribution of elements in Y. The task of communication is for the sender to get his information about Y through to the receiver in terms of the relationships among X and Y as sets of ordered elements. Now if there is no relationship of order between X and Y, then no information can be conveyed. If, on the contrary, there is a determinate and known isomorphism of order (one-to-one correspondence) between X and Y, the receiver knows already what the sender can tell him, and again there is no possible communication of information. Information transfer is possible only when there is a probability relationship between the elements of X and the elements of Y, the nature of which generally is that the occurrence of a given element x_j is neither impossible nor necessary upon the occurrence of a given element y_k. Between any two elements x_j of X and y_k of Y, that is to say, there is a conditional probability, less than unity but greater than zero, that y_k occurs given the occurrence of x_j. If we symbolize the probability that x_j and y_k both occur by '$P(x_j, y_k)$', and the probabilities that x_j and y_k will occur (one without respect to the other) by '$P(x_j)$' and '$P(y_k)$' respectively, then the conditional probability of x_j given y_k is

$$(4) \qquad P(x_j/y_k) = \frac{P(x_j, y_k)}{P(y_k)}$$

The mutual information between x_j and y_k is given by

$$(5) \qquad I(x_j; y_k) = \log \frac{P(x_j/y_k)}{P(x_j)}$$

By a summation similar to that in equation (2)

we finally see that the mutual information between the sets X and Y is just the total of the several mutual information values of each x_j with respect to each y_k, multiplied in each case by the probability of occurrence of that particular combination of x_j and y_k:

(6) $$I(X; Y) = \sum_{X,Y} P(x_j, y_k)\ I(x_j; y_k)$$

$I(X; Y)$ is the average amount of information about X which can be communicated by means of Y, or alternatively (as we shall see) the average amount of information about Y which can be communicated by means of X. Let us interpret these formulae, first in terms of a common code system and then in terms of our example of color constancy.

Consider that X is the ensemble of clicks from a telegraph sounder within earshot of a receiver and that Y is the ensemble of pushes and pulls on a key by means of which a sender enters a message into a telegraphic communication channel. Now if x_1 occurs when and only when y_1 occurs, then the probability $[P(x_1, y_1)]$ of joint occurrence of x_1 and y_1 will be identical both to the probability $[P(y_1)]$ of occurrence of y_1 and to the probability $[P(x_1)]$ of occurrence of x_1. Thus $P(x_1/y_1)$ will be unity, under which condition the receiver can be quite sure that when he receives x_1 on his sounder, y_1 had been entered at the corresponding telegraph key. When errors of transmission enter in, however, $P(y_1)$ will differ from $P(x_1, y_1)$, and the conditional probability $P(x_1/y_1)$ will be less than unity. In this case the mutual information of x_1 with respect to y_1 will be correspondingly less than the self-information of x_1 itself. The self-information of x_1 is an upper bound of the mutual information of x_1 with respect to y_1, since $I(x_1; y_1)$ can never exceed $\log 1/P(x_1)$, which is the self-information of x_1 itself.

The major difference between this interpretation and the one about to be suggested in terms of perceptual patterns is in the "temporal direction" of the relationship between x_j and y_k. Whereas in the telegraphic example y_k precedes x_j (x_j is the indication at the sounder which provides information about what happened at the key, that is, about y_k), in the perceptual example x_j will be the pattern (or color appearance) at t_0 providing information about the appearance y_k which is about to occur at t_1. Since temporal dimensionality is not a factor in the information-theoretic formulae above, there is nothing theoretically objectionable about this shift in direction.[9]

Turning again to the case of color constancy, let us consider what sets the limits on the degree of economy the information-processing system can effect in dealing with changing color phenomena. The principle is that as little information-handling capacity will be expended on a given set of input data as will satisfactorily serve the needs and interests of the percipient. For most purposes very fine distinctions among subtly changing colors are of no pragmatic advantage. But if the percipient's purpose is to maintain a sharp focus on a specific object as it moves against a variegated background, through different degrees of illumination, and so forth, then the percipient must be able to anticipate what color appearance the object will present from one moment to the next, and this anticipation will require more than gross discriminations among primary colors. The degree of discrimination is set by the ongoing success or failure on the part of the percipient in his efforts to follow the object. If he loses the object for a moment, and it is important to find it again, the percipient will stop whatever else he is doing and begin to scrutinize the area where the object last clearly appeared. In the process the percipient will make color discriminations considerably more fine than those which were adequate for his purpose while the object, as it were, was highly visible.

Here there is clearly another principle at work beyond that of generally minimizing the expenditure of information-processing capacity. A percipient will expend as much of his information-processing resources on a changing pattern of sufficient importance as it is necessary to retain his fix upon the pattern. In general, for every pattern in every specific context there is a degree of expectancy set up in the percipient with regard to what is likely to follow the appearance of the pattern itself. If that expectancy is fulfilled, then the mutual information provided by that pattern regarding the other event is high; conversely, if the expectancy is thwarted more or less fully, then the mutual information of that pattern regarding the other event is more or less minimal. Of course for some patterns, such as those in the periphery of our interest, it is not important whether or not they serve well as indicators of future appearances. In such cases a low mutual information level is quite tolerable, and the patterns themselves will be represented in a most vague and inarticulate fashion. For other patterns momentarily at the center of our concern a high degree of fulfilled expectancy is of the essence, and these patterns will be represented in considerable detail. The dynamics of these interactions will be examined in section VI. First however let us examine other basic Gestalt phenomena in terms of our information-theoretic model.

V

Through some ingenious experimental studies Attneave has produced evidence that more information is "concentrated" at points on the border of a figure where the contour changes direction most rapidly.[10] In one experiment subjects were con-

158   *Philosophy and Cybernetics*

fronted with figures including one similar to that below, but without radial lines:

(D)

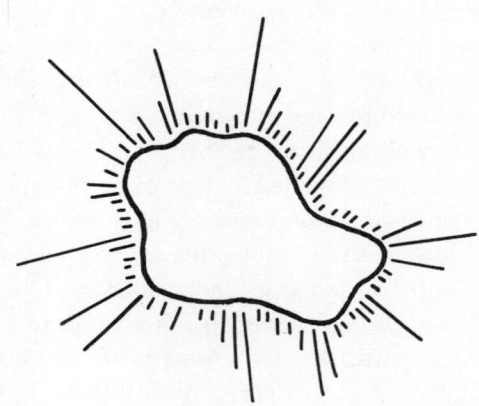

Their instructions were to draw a pattern of 10 dots which would "resemble the shape as closely as possible, and then to indicate on the original outline the exact places which the dots represented."[11] The radial lines in the figure above indicate the relative frequency with which dots were placed on various parts of the contour. As Attneave remarks, the radial lines show considerable agreement among the subjects "in their abstractions of points best representing the shape, and most of these points are taken from regions where the contour is most different from a straight line."[12] The author is consciously unclear about exactly what sort of information is represented in concentration by the radial lines but gives the impression in some passages that he is thinking of what we have termed 'self-information.'[13] If this is his meaning, however, Attneave surely was wrong in his interpretation of his results. If it is the case that the areas of minimum contour are represented in the same grain as the areas of maximum contour, as much information would be required to specify the one in all its detail as to specify the other. According to yet other remarks Attneave seems to be saying rather that the information concentrated at the points of maximum contour is information usable to reproduce the figure overall with good fidelity. "Common objects," he says, "may be represented with great economy, and fairly striking fidelity, by copying the points at which their contours change direction maximally, and then connecting these points appropriately with a straight-edge."[14] Attneave suggests, that is, that one can better reproduce a figure by connecting points of maximum curvature, than by connecting points of minimum curvature, with "neutral" straight lines. But this suggestion also is wrong. To see this the reader may first select the ten points on the contour of the figure above which are associated with the longest radial lines and then carefully select ten other points from among those associated with the shortest radial lines. If this is done on tracing paper or in some other fashion to allow direct comparison of the two resulting reproductions, the reader will find (at least if he chose points close to those chosen by the present author) that the two reproductions are almost equally faithful to the original; the one connecting the minimal points might even turn out better. It appears then that although Attneave is intuitively right in saying that more information is concentrated at points of maximum curvature, the sense of 'information' in which this is correct is not yet clear.

According to the present analysis there are two senses in which information might be said to be concentrated at points of maximum curvature on a figure, both different from either sense discussed in the paragraph above. The first sense has to do with the self-information of the elements in the figure. The sense is simply this: as $I(X)$ decreases for the figure overall, points of maximum contour are processed in proportionately greater detail than are points of minimum contour. The reason for this concerns the second sense, namely, that the areas of maximum contour provide greater mutual information with regard to the structure of patterns yet to appear. In the case of a child's "spiker" top, for example, the appearance in one's perceptual field of the sharply pointed aspect of the toy is more indicative of what is likely to appear in subsequent moments of perception than is the appearance of one of the various rounded portions of the object. The reason, in common sense terms, is merely that there are more round objects (balls, knobs, bat tops, and so on) likely to appear in the neighborhood of a child than there are likely objects with pointed contours. Thus the appearance of the latter is a better indication of further appearances of a top forthcoming than is the appearance of a rounded contour. In general, sharp and unusual contours are rendered in greater detail by the processes of perception than are smooth and common contours, and the reason is that the mutual information of the former aspects is generally greater than that of the latter. The information-processing system, as it were, has "learned" this fact from "experience" and proceeds accordingly whenever the option is presented of processing this or that aspect of a configuration in more or less detail.

We are brought closer to the role of "perceptual learning" in the structuring of patterns by a brief consideration of the so-called "alternating," or "double-aspect," figures celebrated by Gestalt psychologists. Rubin's vase-face is famous among such figures.[15]

Now it is clear that a subject not familiar with vases could not (or would not) see the ambiguous figure as a vase, while another subject (imaginatively conceived) who has seen vases but never faces would see it only as a vase, This suggests that both aspects of the "alternating" figure must be rather common to the subject who experiences a natural and easy shift of attention from one aspect to the other. Another noteworthy feature of the "alternating figure" phenomenon is that no appreciably greater effort of attention is required to focus upon one aspect of the figure than upon the other. This suggests that both aspects are rendered at about the same level of detail by the mechanisms of perceptual consciousness.[16] The explanation of the "alternating figure" phenomenon, then, seems to be that two ways of rendering a given set of data are equally likely, and hence perceptually competitive, when (1) both renditions yield patterns of approximately equal value in terms of mutual information in the percipient's perceptual environment and (2) both renditions can be accomplished with approximately the same expenditure of information-processing capacity, that is, with approximately equal self-information involved in the resulting patterns. Only when both conditions are present will a given configuration appear as an easily reversible "alternating" figure.

It is undoubtedly true that some patterns appear with greater rapidity than others in the context of a given perceptual field. To say this is not to allude to the obvious fact that some objects appear more *often* than others; it is to suggest rather that a given subject's perceptual set may be such that he is more likely to see objects in a given field in terms of some patterns than in terms of others.[17] A man in his living room, for example, at first glance will be very ready to take an appropriately situated object as a chair and very unlikely to take it as a bear. What is true for the first glance, of course, may not hold for the second. If the object is in fact a bear, unaccountably squatting where his arm chair usually is situated, then upon taking the inevitable second look the man will experience a radical alteration in his perceptual field. If, on the other hand, the object he had expected to see had been replaced by a familiar table, he might note the presence of the table after an initial moment of mild curiosity and go his way without thinking more of the matter. Since tables and chairs, but not bears, are common living-room furniture, one is perceptually prepared to encounter them and does so without a break in the normal smooth flow of objects in and out of his perceptual field. The appearance of a bear, however, would not be integrated into one's perception of a living-room situation without conscious effort.

We have already encountered two scales of priority along which patterns might be ordered for service in the articulation of a subject's perceptual field. First is the ordering of patterns according to mutual information, which gives high priority to patterns which most often and most readily provide continuity between past and future moments of a subject's perceptual experience. This ordering of course changes with context. Table and chair patterns have a higher priority than bear and tree patterns for living-room contexts but not in the context of a forest, and vases hold the edge over faces in an expensive pottery shop but not in a movie theatre. The second ordering is with respect to survival value or some other matter essential for continued well-being. When the figure of a bear appears in one's perceptual field, it takes precedence over practically any other appearance in practically any context (save in a zoo where we unquestioningly expect all strange things to be caged). Yet another ordering has to do with the so-called "basic desires" of the subject organism, the priority varying here with the condition of the subject and his recent history. A hungry man will more likely see food objects than will a man recently fed, while a man past seventy will fixate less frequently than a man of twenty upon contours in his environment suggestive of the feminine form.

Other priority orderings also undoubtedly are operative in the guidance of our pattern-formation mechanisms from context to context; the botanist, for example, will dwell on flowers in situations where the hunter will seek signs of game. But it is pointless for the moment to attempt to provide a general characterization of interacting priority systems operating in the structuring of an agent's perceptual field. And it is pointless as well to speculate where (if anywhere) in the labyrinth of the nervous system these patterns thus ordered are stored. Let us be content merely with the observation that there must be a system of priority ratings among anticipated patterns in a given perceptual context, which vary of course from context to context and from person to person, and that patterns of high priority will more readily be deployed in the ongoing structuring of the perceptual field.[18]

This concept of a priority ranking among possible patterns is coupled in the following section with the concepts of self-information and of mutual information, and a quantitative account of the dynamics of pattern formation in perceptual consciousness is tentatively advanced.

VI

A shift in attention often brings new figures into the perceptual field and brings out new relations among figures previously under survey. The structure of these changing views varies moreover with the situation of the viewer and with the pattern-types most prominent in his concern. I wish now to articulate a general conjecture regarding the dynamics of pattern formation in terms of which these observations can be interpreted with considerable intuitive fidelity.

The elements have been introduced. They include (1) the self-information $[I(X)]$ of a pattern or ensemble X, (2) the mutual information $[I(X; Y)]$ of X with respect to Y, and (3) the priority of a given configuration X at a given moment in perceptual consciousness. Let us designate the priority (ranking) of X by the symbol 'R_x'. The conjecture is that information is processed by the nervous system according to the following general relationship:

(7) $$I(X) = \frac{R_x}{I(X; Y)}$$

If $I(X)$ is the amount of information-processing

capacity of the agent expended on X, resulting in a given degree of articulation of the configuration, and if $I(X; Y)$ is the tendency of X to lead to successful anticipations by the agent of important details in his perceptual environment, then equation (7) asserts that the degree of articulation of a given pattern (i) will vary inversely with the degree of integrative power of this pattern and (ii) will vary directly with the priority attached to the pattern by the agent in the context in question. R_x is a constant which however will represent different values for different persons in different contexts. $I(X)$ generally will be interpreted as dependent and $I(X; Y)$ as independent variables, although there is no reason in principle why this relationship might not be reversed.

As a concession to ordinary language, let us continue the practice (already surreptitiously begun) of referring to $I(X)$ as the degree of attention expended on the configuration X. It might be suggested that as a matter of fact the varying degrees of attention which one is quite conscious of exerting on various objects are nothing more or less than variations in the amount of information-processing capacity expended on a pattern at a given moment of consciousness. If this is correct, then we have in $I(X)$ a measure of attention, awareness, or consciousness, as the reader wills. It seems intuitively apparent both that we are attentive only to patterns which are presented with a high level of articulation and, on the other hand, that we cannot render a configuration in detail without devoting considerable attention to it. For purposes of informal discussion let us interpret $I(X)$ in terms of attention, or awareness. If this disturbs the reader, he can always translate back into information-theoretic terms without losing the drift of the discussion.

Interpretation of $I(X)$ as a measure of attention has one noteworthy consequence which appears to be more than a convenient metaphor. Since presumably the information-handling capacity of a given percipient at any given moment is finite,[19] there must be an upper bound to the degree of attention that can be expended momentarily upon a given pattern. Various channels of activity might compete for this capacity from moment to moment. Thus when there is a call for concentrated attention from a quarter other than perception, or from a fresh area within the perceptual field, the percipient's attention will be shifted away from the object previously of immediate perceptual concern. The case of the bear in the living room provides an illustration.

Let 'X' in equation (7) represent the appearance of the bear and 'Y' represent other appearances which the subject will be concerned to integrate or reconcile with X during simultaneous and immediately subsequent moments of perception. 'R_x' represents the priority or degree of urgency with which the information-processing system of the subject will react to X. Since the appearance of a bear almost anywhere outside of a zoo is a matter of considerable concern, a high value will attach to R_x during initial moments of perception. And since by and large any unexpected and startling appearance in a given context is, by virtue of being unexpected, at first hard to integrate with other more commonplace appearances within that context, a low value initially will attach to $I(X; Y)$. Both variables therefore contribute to an initially high value for $I(X)$, and this sudden demand on the subject's attention typically would cause him to drop any other perceptual concern he may have had during the moments preceding. In other words, since the appearance of a bear in the living room is both highly unexpected and of top concern, the subject's attention at first will be wholly absorbed by that appearance. His attention will be fixated on the bear. But prudence demands that his attention almost immediately be commanded by an effective avoidance routine. So unless the subject is mesmerized by the presence of danger, the structure of his perceptual field will undergo a second radical change during the next few moments. If the bear is stationary, he will seek immediately to account for this and to determine whether its immobility can be relied upon to continue (his perceptual field will change radically once again when he realizes the animal is stuffed, and R_x will sharply decrease). Or if the bear is moving towards the subject, he will have detected the directional tendency of motion and begun to act accordingly. $I(X; Y)$ in this case will be on the increase, since he can begin to anticipate the animal's movement, but $I(X)$ will remain high because of the high value yet attached to R_x. As the subject's attention subsequently becomes devoted to escape or to the capture of the bear however, the priority allowed to the bear-appearance might shift to another set of patterns, such as a sticky window latch or a box of revolver shells, and $I(X)$ will decrease considerably as the bear-appearance slips for the moment into the periphery of the subject's perceptual field. Only when the future movements of the bear are entirely predictable, yielding high $I(X; Y)$, and when R_x has decreased to a level merely of lively interest, will $I(X)$ stabilize at a normally constant value.

Next consider various situations in which the priority assigned X is middling or low. Travelers approaching the Rocky Mountains along a road from the plains seem often to be puzzled by the first appearance of snow-covered peaks before they come clearly into view. Is it smoke drifting away from a nearby industrial area? Apparently not, for it seems less amorphous than one would expect smoke to appear from that distance. Unable to integrate the appearance with other aspects of his perceptual field (low $I(X; Y)$), although only mildly concerned with its identity (middling R_x), the percipient turns with closer attention (high $I(X)$) to scrutinize the general locale of the puzzling appearance. Finally he realizes that the form is that of a snow-covered highland which is suggestive from the distance of a low-lying and stable cloud. Since the mountain-appearance integrates well with the remainder of his perceptual field, with a resulting increase in $I(X; Y)$, $I(X)$ soon will decrease to a level compatible with leisurely aesthetic appreciation. When the percipient "forgets" the mountains and turns the focus of his attention to other things, the mountain-appearance might nonetheless remain well-integrated at the boundaries of his perceptual field. $I(X)$ now will be minimal. Such is the case in general with ill-defined Gestalts which we barely notice because of their smooth integration with other appearances in moments of well-ordered perception. At the extreme are configurations of no immediate interest to the percipient, which consequently have self-information values approaching zero. Such occur typically within the phenomenal field of someone deeply involved in thought or merely daydreaming. So too is the case with nocturnal rest, when the priorities of daily concern are set aside. Only a privileged few perceptual patterns reach awareness through external sensory channels. The few among these that integrate well (the baby's cry) receive a low but appreciable value of $I(X)$ and are acted upon in due time, while those which get through with poor integration (a bang on the front door) might cause a startled reaction with high $I(X)$ comparable to that accompanying the appearance of the bear.

$I(X; Y)$, which takes on values through the

A MODEL OF PATTERN FORMATION 171

operation of influctuant skills of perceptual organization, is always a considerable factor in the determination of $I(X)$. The influence of R_x, on the other hand, often can be controlled and even eliminated. Most of the figural demonstrations of Gestalt phenomena suitable for illustration in textbooks are of a sort in which motivation is not a consideration and in which $I(X)$ consequently takes on values merely as an inverse function of $I(X; Y)$. An interesting example is in the perceptual "saturation" induced by fixating one's attention for an

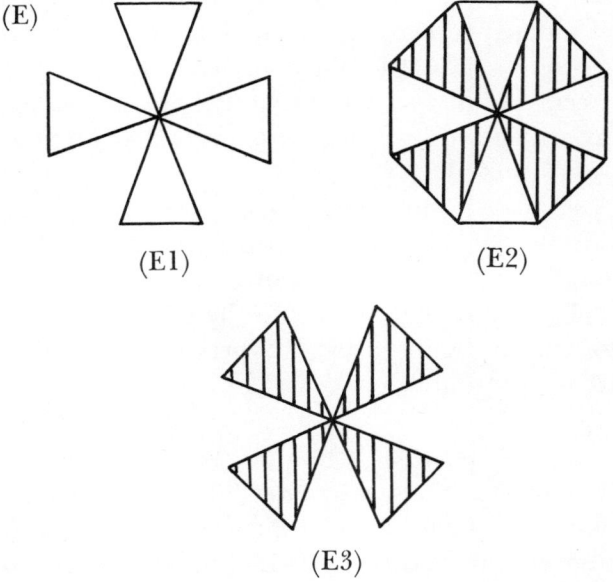

(E)

(E1) (E2)

(E3)

extended time upon a figure in isolation (either E1 or E3), which then recedes when viewed with other shapes in a context of figure-ground ambiguity (E2).[20] The dominance of one form (X) in the center pattern, after prolonged fixation by the percipient on the other, can be explained in terms of equation (7) above. Since R_x here is constant, $I(X)$ is a function solely of the degree of integration of X in the percipient's patterned awareness from moment to moment. While the percipient's attention is fixated on X, this integration is high, and $I(X; Y)$ tends to maximum value. $I(X)$ thus tends to decrease, and the pattern becomes a relatively inarticulate outline. The subject may even feel obliged to exert effort in order to retain his focus on the pattern. When attention is shifted to the center configuration however, novel shapes appear which require integrating with the familiar form of preceding moments. The self-information of the novel form thus will be temporarily high, while that of the familiar form remains low. The novel form consequently stands out in degree of detail and comes to dominate the combined presentation as figure over the previously familiar pattern as ground.

VII

Let us turn finally to some interesting mathematical consequences of equation (7) above. A significant property of mutual information between X and Y is its reciprocity. That is,

(8) $$I(X; Y) = I(Y; X)$$

A MODEL OF PATTERN FORMATION

To account for this reciprocity in terms of our examples, consider once again the case of the bear behind the chair. An expansion of (8) yields

$$(9) \quad \sum_{X,Y} \log \frac{(Px_j/y_k)}{P(x_j)} = \sum_{Y,X} \log \frac{(Py_k/x_j)}{P(y_k)}$$

For perspicuity we may rewrite this as

$$(10) \quad \log \frac{P(X/Y)}{P(X)} = \log \frac{P(Y/X)}{P(Y)}$$

What needs to be shown is the equivalence in our interpretation between the conditional probability of X given Y, divided by the probability of X, and the conditional probability of Y given X, divided by the probability of Y. Consider 'X' to represent the appearance of a bear and chair at t_1, and 'Y' to represent the appearance merely of a chair at t_0. $P(X)$ is quite low in the context of our example, while $P(Y)$ correspondingly is quite high. $P(X/Y)$, as a matter of common expectancy, is also very low indeed, while $P(Y/X)$ correspondingly is very high. This may be seen by reflecting on the rendition of the latter two expressions: $P(X/Y)$ is the expectancy of a bear-appearance associated with a chair-appearance at t_1 if only the appearance of a chair at t_0 is given, while $P(Y/X)$ is the expectancy that a chair did appear at t_0 if it is given that a bear and a chair appear at t_1. $P(X/Y)$ is low because we do not expect to find bears behind chairs in living rooms; let us arbitrarily assign it the value 1/100. $P(Y/X)$ is high because we just do not see both bears and chairs appearing from nowhere. If there is a bear and a chair at t_1, there very likely is a chair at t_0 (very likely also that there is a bear at t_0, which there was not; but this consideration does not enter into the interpretation). Let us assign the value unity to $P(Y/X)$. Finally we will assign 1/10 as the value of $P(Y)$, the likelihood that a chair will appear in the subject's perception of the living room. Since the likelihood of a bear behind a chair is equal to the product of the probability of a bear appearing with a chair and that of a chair appearing alone, the value of $P(X)$ is 1/1000. Substituting these values in (10), we have an equality which satisfies both the mathematical requirements and common intuitions regarding what is likely and what is not.

A further mathematical consequence of (7) which warrants brief note is the fact that $I(X)$ goes to zero along with R_x. One pays no attention to something in which one finds no interest. On the other hand, we would not want to say that $I(X)$ becomes infinitely large as $I(X; Y)$ goes to zero. We should say, rather, that the question of attention level just does not arise in connection with patterns which are totally without integrative capacity in our perceptual field.

A final remark returns us to the concern of the opening pages. It follows as a basic requirement of information theory that *only* data which to some extent are integrated within patterns can serve as the basis for sound expectancies regarding the future of a subject's perceptual field. When X is entirely random, then P(X; Y) is equal to P(X), which is to say that I(X; Y) is zero:

$$(11) \quad I(X; Y) = \log \frac{P(X; Y)}{P(X)}$$

$$= \log 1$$

$$= 0$$

Given that some degree of organization into patterns is a necessary function of a data-processing system capable of prediction, it is worthwhile to conjecture further along the lines suggesting this requirement. Attneave has remarked that sensory events "are highly interdependent in both space and time; if we know at a given moment the states of a limited number of receptors . . . we can make better-than-chance inferences with respect to the prior and subsequent states of these receptors, and also with respect to the present, prior, and subsequent states of other receptors."[21] Other investigators have found a direct relationship between the amount of informaton in a pattern and the degree of attention it elicits.[22] The effort in this study has been to attach quantitative interpretations to these insights from the point of view of the requirements of an information-processing system of the sort we may presume active within the human organism. This at least is a necessary ingredient in a useful quantitative model of the dynamics of pattern formation in consciousness.

NOTES

1. See, for example, F. H. Allport, *Theories of Perception and the Concept of Structure* (New York: Holt, Rinehart and Winston, 1959); D. Krech and R. S. Crutchfield, *Elements of Psychology* (New York: Knopf, 1959), Chap. 5; and D. E. Berlyne, *Structure and Direction in Thinking* (New York: Wiley, 1965).
2. H. Dreyfus, "Alchemy and Artificial Intelligence," *Rand Report P-3244* (1965), part 3.
3. A critique of the assimilation of recognition to classification may be found in the present author's *Recognition: A Study in the Philosophy of Artificial Intelligence* (Notre Dame: University of Notre Dame Press, 1965).
4. The classic treatment of information theory is found in C. E. Shannon and W. Weaver, *The Mathematical Theory of Communication* (Urbana: University of Illinois Press, 1949). Several useful texts on the subject have recently appeared, such as N. Abramson, *Information Theory and Coding* (New York: McGraw-Hill, 1963). A brief introduction to the basic concepts of information theory, with a minimum of technical expressions, may be found in Chapter 11 of K. Sayre, *Recognition: A Study in the Philosophy of Artificial Intelligence.*
5. Logarithms to the base 2 are customarily used in the measure of information. For an explanation of this the reader may refer to any of the works cited in the previous footnote.
6. Recent studies have shown that in situations of boredom or of sensory deprivation an organism will seek additional stimulation or even will expand on

present stimulation through hallucination. A review of empirical studies in this regard may be found in D. E. Berlyne, "Curiosity and Exploration," *Science*, 153, 3731 (July 1, 1966), 25–33.

7. F. Attneave, *Applications of Information Theory to Psychology* (New York: Holt, Rinehart and Winston, 1959), p. 82.

8. *Ibid.*, p. 83 [author's italics].

9. That temporal directionality is not a factor is obvious in the proof that $I(x_j; y_k)$ is equal to $I(y_k; x_j)$:

$$I(x_j; y_k) = \log\frac{P(x_j/y_k)}{P(x_j)}$$

$$= \log\frac{P(x_j, y_k)}{P(y_k)P(x_j)}$$

$$= \log\frac{P(y_k, x_j)}{P(x_j)P(y_k)}$$

$$= \log\frac{P(y_k/x_j)}{P(y_k)}$$

$$= I(y_k; x_j)$$

10. Attneave's study is reported in "Some Informational Aspects of Visual Perception," *Psychological Review*, 61, 3 (1954), 183–93.

11. *Loc. cit.*, p. 185.

12. *Ibid.*

13. Elsewhere in the article Attneave speaks of "homogenous," or minimal, slope as being redundant, and in the same sentence he goes on to suggest that information is "concentrated at those points on a contour at which its direction changes most rapidly . . . ." *Ibid.*, p. 184.

14. *Ibid.*, p. 185.

15. Other common and very striking examples are the "duck-rabbit" (L. Wittgenstein, *Philosophical Investigations* [New York: Macmillan, 1953], p. 194) and the "girl-hag" (R. W. Leeper, *Journal of Genetic Psychology*, 46 [1935], 41).

16. The initial difficulty people sometimes experience in "seeing" both aspects of more complicated "alternating" figures, such as the "wife"–"mother-in-law," has to do with uncertainty as to level of detail significant in the perception of one or another of the aspects.

17. Krech and Crutchfield (*op. cit.*, p. 101) show a figure in which a pirate and a rabbit can be seen with equal ease but which follows in the normal scansion of the page a similar figure in which the pirate form is far more dominant. One thus first sees the neutral figure with the pirate form to the fore. In subsequent text, however, the authors suggest that the figure also exhibits a rabbit form. A subsequent glance with this new mental set easily reveals a rabbit to the reader.

18. As Berlyne remarks ("Curiosity and Exploration," *loc. cit.*, p. 30), "The motivational effects of collative stimulus properties are by no means confined to occasioning and directing exploratory responses. They include the factors making for 'good' or 'bad' form, which were shown by the Gestalt psychologists to govern many perceptual phenomena." See also C. O. Williams, "Some Evidence for a Hierarchy of Needs," *The Journal of General Psychology*, 70 (1964), 85–88.

19. Efforts have been made by engineering psychologists to measure the informational capacities of human sensory channels. See, for example, J. W. Sender, "Human Performance," *International Science and Technology*, 55 (July 1966), 58–68.

20. See Krech and Crutchfield, *op. cit.,* p. 109, with credits therein to Boring, Langfeld, and Weld, *Foundations of Psychology* (New York: Wiley, 1948).
21. *Loc. cit.,* p. 183.
22. See *ibid.*

III. On Certain Capacities in Men and Machines

MEMORY, MODELS, AND MEANING

F. J. Crosson

When the histologist looks at the brain, he sees something which is very reminiscent of large electronic computers. He sees a small number of basic components repeated over and over again. All the complexity lies in the innumerable interconnections, not in the basic components. . . . Thus if one is to study the physiological background of memory one might start with such a model of interconnected neurons. We do not claim that the model is altogether true, but it is simple, and presents itself on the basis of anatomical data. There is no anatomical evidence for a storage organ used to file away the immense amount of information, which every person retains in his memory.[1]

ELSASSER HERE SPEAKS OF AN ANATOMICAL model of the brain, that is, one couched in terms of neurological elements and their interrelations, which, while not verified by the present data of research, seems promising as a guide to further inquiry. McCulloch and Pitts develop a formal model of neural nets based on the logical structure of finite automata, a model which aims both at unifying neurological and automata theory and at orienting the work of computer technologists on mechanical simulation of brain functions. Presupposed to the implementation of both of these kinds of models is another: a conceptual model of the functions which are being investigated or simulated. A model of this kind attempts by analysis of those functions to lay out with precision the structure of what is being modeled. In the case of memory a conceptual model would be an attempt to specify the logical (rather than the material) conditions for calling certain instances of behavior "remembering" and also to sort out the diverse kinds of behavior to which the term is applied.

That there is diversity is attested by the fact that while storage or retention is thought of as a common condition for memory, psychologists regularly distinguish between retrieval, recognition, learning, and recall (among other categories). That there is confusion about the differentiation is attested by references to the memory of a stone or a chemical compound,[2] whereas cyberneticians regularly refer to memory in a univocal fashion when speaking of simulation.[3] No doubt this sort of reference is induced by the fact that in present-day computers and automata the so-called memory or storage component is uniform in its operation, but equally doubtless is the fact that the use of the generic term 'memory' is misleading if not confusing.

Psychology is less help here than one might expect, since psychologists are less interested in the criteria of memory attribution than in the empirical conditions of its exercise: particular features describable in terms of span of retention, proactive and retroactive inhibitions, memory curves, and so on. Hence the same general categories referred to above tend to be assumed and repeated by subsequent experimenters without much attempt to uncover subgroupings of kinds of memory. To put this in another and perhaps less meretricious-sounding way, the different senses of memory are presupposed by the experimenter and are not themselves to be established experimentally. This does not in the least affect the validity of experimental results; what it does affect is the meaning or the bearing of these results on the formal models of the brain, and more pertinently on efforts to simulate mechanically the function in question.

I

A brief look at a tentative schema for the categorization of kinds of memory will provide an illustration of the materials which could be used in the development of a conceptual model.

Among the distinguishable varieties of memory several have already been, or are in process of being, mechanically simulated.

Storage or retention, as the capacity to reproduce

information on demand, is embodied in present computers. A more elaborate form of this is a computer programmed to reply to a variety of factual questions, a frequent display at fairs and exhibitions. *Recognition* in the form of many types of pattern-recognition machines is no longer news in the literature, although the distinction of recognition and classification is far from being generally realized.[4] *Learning,* as a change in the probability of a given response, is exemplified in self-adaptive mechanisms, which again, although more developed in theory than in the laboratory, are no longer a novelty in the literature.

But in spite of the general admission of *recall,* or redintegration, the capacity to advert in some fashion to past events, there has been thus far no attempt made to simulate it. This is the more remarkable in that recall is perhaps the most typical function of memory.

This grouping into simulated memory operations and those not yet simulated is paralleled in the distinction among the verbal forms in which they are expressed. Remembering, in the sense of retention or recognizing or of having learned, is always paraphrasable by the verb 'to know.' To have learned to ride a bicycle or to remember the flag of the United States or to remember who discovered America is to know how (to do something) or to know (someone or something) or to know that (such-and-such is the case). But remembering Joan crying is not just knowing that Joan cried. It represents a claim to have had direct experience of the event and to have now some kind of access to that experience which is neither a relearning nor a recognizing of it.

It is worth noting that the verb 'to know' signifies a capacity or disposition to act; in using it (as in the above paraphrases) we do not assert that the subject is doing something but that he can or could under certain conditions exhibit a certain kind of behavior. Conversely, in saying that Peter recalls Joan crying we do refer to the exercise of a capacity to recall.

This distinction can be sharpened by putting it in the following way. Where the verb 'to remember' is followed by 'that p' (where 'p' designates a proposition), by 'how to A' (where 'A' designates a description of behavior), or by 'x' (where 'x' represents a noun phrase designating a place, event, or thing), it conveys no more than the use of the verb 'to know' plus the implication of a significant time lapse since the knowledge was last exercised, whether the exercise be reproducing information, exhibiting behavior, or recognizing. Thus while "I remember how to drive a car" would be uninformative under ordinary circumstances, it could become informative if I have not driven a car for many years. I do not remember my phone number; I know it. I do not remember (recognize) my wife when I see her in the morning, but this does not mean that I do not know her; it means that to speak of recognizing her under such circumstances would be bizarre, meaningless. But to say I remember Joan crying is to claim more than that I know Joan cried (although it entails this) and that I have not "reactivated" this awareness for some time: it adds to these the claims (1) to have had direct awareness of the event referred to and (2) to have access to that experience now.

Another way to reinforce the distinction between these subgroups is to consider the role played by images. For the exercise of learned behavior, for the reproduction of stored information, for the recognition of the previously known, advertence to images normally plays no role. Recourse to images in these cases is indicative rather of a deficiency in the functioning of memory. For recall, on the other hand, advertence to one's images is usual rather than unusual. Hence we find the use of terms like 'vivid,' 'lively,' 'vague' for recall, whereas one does not vividly remember who discovered America.[5]

Finally, contrary to what might seem at first thought to be the case, recall is the memory function least susceptible to explanation by a trace or engram theory. For it is not reducible to the retrieval of information from storage or the exercise of a learned pattern of behavior, since these operations are normally not accompanied by any awareness of or advertence to past experience in their execution. One can retrieve *The Star-Spangled Banner* from storage without any awareness—perhaps without even being able to recall—where or when or even that he has sung it before.

Nor does mere reactivation of the trace seem to be a sufficient ground for recall, in spite of Eccles' remark: "the remembered thought appears in consciousness as soon as its specific space-time schema is replayed in the brain cortex."[6] Wilder Penfield's remarkable reactivation of past experiences through stimulation of the temporal lobes does not seem to meet Eccles' criterion. In Penfield's words:

> . . . the patients have never looked upon an experiential response as a remembering. Instead of that it is a hearing-again and a seeing-again—a living-through moments of past time.[7]

Recall appears then to be distinct from the activation of behavior by stored information and from the reactivation of that stored information itself. Recall is not simply knowing how to or that (plus a time lapse) nor is it re-experiencing the past—"the remembered sun doesn't shine."

II

A new and relatively unexplored approach to the development of a model of memory is offered by the application of information theory to the analysis of epistemic processes.

Even the simplest perception has meaning or signification in the sense that it points beyond itself; it implicitly profers other sides or aspects or perspectives which are not yet given to us explicitly. There is a constellation of "cross references" in the given percept which lead us to expect or anticipate what other aspects of the perceived object will be like. The British psychologist Bartlett has expressed this by saying that every perception has an inferential structure; we might say the explicitly given is the protasis and the adumbrated aspects are the apodosis. There are determinate and determinable elements involved in our perceptual experiences.

Information theory distinguishes sharply between information and meaning, between, we might say, the semiotic problem and the semantic problem.[8] Information is measured by the entropy or freedom of a message source in its choice of symbols to be emitted. If anything at all might be sent, the probability (P) of any given symbol-event (E) is low, and its information

$$I(E) = \log_2 \frac{1}{P(E)}$$

is therefore correspondingly high. For a zero-memory information source the average amount of information per symbol, H(S), for a set of messages is

$$H(S) = \sum_S P(s_i) \log_2 \frac{1}{P(s_i)}$$

But if the information source is an ergodic Markoff source,[9] then there are constraints imposed on the output sequences. The probability of a given symbol being emitted is a function of the already emitted symbols; that is, its probability may be calculated from a knowledge of the conditional symbol probabilities. For an mth order Markoff source the probability of emitting a given symbol is a function of the preceding m symbols (called the state of the system):

$$P(s_i/s_{j_1}, s_{j_2}, \ldots, s_{j_m})$$

and here the average information or entropy is

$$H(S/s_{j_1}, s_{j_2}, \ldots, s_{j_m}) =$$
$$\sum_S P(s_i/s_{j_1}, s_{j_2}, \ldots, s_{j_m}) \log_2 \frac{1}{P(s_i/s_{j_1}, s_{j_2}, \ldots, s_{j_m})}$$

The constraint which is imposed on the output sequence by the conditional probabilities limits the maximum possible entropy (or freedom of choice) of the source and consequently decreases the information conveyed by the actual choice. The ratio of the actual entropy to the maximum possible entropy—a ratio called the 'relative entropy'—decreases, and conversely the redundancy (1 minus the relative entropy) increases. As the entropy (or dis-ordered choice) decreases, order increases, and thus entropy is associated with information as redundancy is associated with order. We may then relate order with meaning or meaningfulness by the intuitive hypothesis suggested in such phrases as William James' "blooming, buzzing confusion." This hypothesis will allow us to distinguish clearly between information and meaning and also allow us to relate them illuminatingly.

D. M. McKay[10] has defined the meaning of an indicative item of information as the selective function which it exercises on the set or range of the receiver's possible states of orientation (transition probability matrices). If we translate this into psychological terms, it states that the meaning of an item of information is the *Aufgabe,* or set of expectancies, which it elicits in the perceiver. When we can anticipate, when we "know what to expect," we find the event or situation meaningful. But since we normally have no experience, no feeling of expectancy in perception, perhaps it is better to avoid using psychological terms and say rather that our perceptual field at any given moment presents us with objects under particular aspects, wholes partially presented. The not-yet-explicitly-given aspects of the object constitute the *meaning* of the given unitary aspect, so that we do not perceive merely a red surface but the brick wall of a building.

By extrapolation this suggested relation between information and meaning would lead us to expect that under conditions of maximum information or entropy, where the *quale* of the perceptual field is statistically independent over time (James' "blooming, buzzing confusion"), the meaning would approach zero. Conversely, where the redundancy approached 100 per cent—no surprises, all anticipations fulfilled—the information yielded by successive moments would approach zero. It is interesting to remark on the basis of the sensory deprivation experiments[11] that the latter situation would seem to be as humanly intolerable as the former and that subjects begin spontaneously to introduce novelty into the flow of perceptions (delusions, memories, and so on).

Psychological evidence seems to confirm the hypothesis that the perceptual process is more correlated with meaning (in the above sense) than with information for both static and transitional moments of the process. As the work of Attneave, Hochberg, and others[12] has shown, at any given moment the innate patterns so emphasized by Gestalt psychology reflect the tendency of organisms to perceive in terms of figures of maximum redundancy. Moreover, the Gestalt factors (such as symmetry, simplicity, closure, good continuation, and such) are all effective in establishing the solidity or substantiality of objects, a substantiality which we stubbornly persist in perceiving, as the "constancies" of shape, color, size, and so forth indicate. In general "the probability of a given perceptual response to a stimulus is an inverse function of the amount of information needed to specify it."[13]

For patterns whose relevance for the organism is learned the *Aufgabe,* or "set," of course increases the probability of the stimulus evoking a particular perceptual response and of other stimuli being treated as noise or irrelevant. Once the transition probabilities are set up (whatever be the neural or electrical basis: lowering of thresholds, linkages firing together, and such) within and between sensory modalities, the perceptual protentions or anticipations tend to suppress or obliterate stimuli which do not fit into the redundancy-structured Markoff process. This is why, for example, it is so easy to miss misprints.

The consequences of this characterization of perception in terms of meaning for a theory of memory are clear. It suggests that this perceptual data processing greatly reduces the quantity of information needed for memory, since the input has been stripped or reduced by filter patterns. This means that our memories must be highly schematic compared to the original input, but there is ample psychological and neurological evidence that this is the case.

This is why we remember the meanings in last night's newspaper story without being able to recall more than a few key words. The redundancy of the English text which facilitates our easy apprehension of it also enables us to reconstruct its sense by filling in gaps with our own words from a few key elements, just as is the case of our memories of plays, movies, concerts, and so forth. It is not merely familiarity with the works of Mozart which makes a theme of his easier to remember or recognize than one of Alban Berg; in terms of probability frequencies Mozart is much more redundant than Berg, whose music is almost random.[14] We might say that memory normally functions in a *oratio obliqua* mode, by storing the gist of what was said or done, rather than *oratio recta,* the actual words or events.[15]

What MacKay calls the set of transition or conditional probability matrices therefore corresponds to a set of memories in the sense of storage retention,[16] which are pattern rules that not merely handle redundancy in the Markoff-process of perception but also impose a structure of redundancy on perception.

Such a theory of the logical structure of memory traces—although not developed in terms of information theory—may be glimpsed in the Gestaltist's experiments on the "dynamism" of traces.[17] These experiments showed that over a period of time memories of perceived patterns tended to "normalize" themselves, that is, to shift spontaneously in the direction of simpler or more regular (hence redundant) patterns. The generalization suggested by these findings is that storage in memory tends to be in the form of typically meaningful patterns which are stripped of irrelevant elements.

III

There is however a large gap in the materials thus far laid out for a comprehensive model of memory, and that is the area of the "pathology" of memory: forgetting. It is worth remarking that there are few, if any, models which incorporate a prominent place for forgetting aside from the somewhat limited consideration of the decay of the memory trace. The latter model is limited both because it would seem to apply if at all only to short-term memory and because there is as yet no persuasive evidence, only the barest hints, of any specific engram structure (whether macromolecules, reverberating circuits, or whatever). Psychologically there seems to be ground for distinguishing a short-term memory (I remember what I had for breakfast this morning, but not what I had last week), but at the same time subjects under hypnosis and in psychoanalytic therapy can recall details of long-ago events with remarkable precision. This suggests that our storage far exceeds our normal retrieval capacity and raises questions about the significance of any decay theory.

Moreover, forgetting seems to be less the loss of a trace (engram) than the loss of the place (address) where the memory is stored. Our attempt to remember is "blocked." The questions "How do blocks occur?" "How can they be avoided?" and so forth are psychological questions. The conceptual questions relate to the necessary and sufficient conditions for the truth or falsity of the statement that John has forgotten.

Among the necessary conditions are (1) that x was learned or experienced in the past, (2) that x is not now accessible, (3) that (1) and (2) are both known by the one who makes the assertion. This last condition means that the statement that someone has forgotten x always entails the claim to remember not only what is forgotten but also that it was previously known. The lack of accessibility mentioned under condition (2) may of course be either of short or long duration, temporary or permanent.

The stipulation of accessibility has another important consequence. It relates to the fact, mentioned above, that forgetting is primarily an inability to retrieve the information rather than a loss of the trace. The neurological verification of a memory trace (assuming we could isolate and identify such a thing) would not of itself constitute sufficient grounds for claiming that someone remembers or has not forgotten.

The question of a sufficient set of conditions raises some puzzles. If we could specify the behavior which would constitute grounds sufficient for saying 'he has forgotten,' then such behavior could in principle be simulated by a machine. But this seems paradoxical because it makes forgetting something to be done rather than the failure to do something. In psychoanalytic theory there is a kind of "deliberate" forgetting (repression), but even there forgetting is not something which a person can reasonably be directed to do. (Suggestion under hypnosis is quite different and deserves separate examination in this regard.) In fact the command to forget such-and-such normally has the opposite consequence.

These puzzles and others reflect the paucity of attention which has been given to forgetting as a specific phenomenon. Present models of memory all lack an adequate place for it.[18]

IV

To sum up, it would appear that all remembering of the first three kinds (knowing that, knowing how, recognizing) is a knowing, and we can always substitute for the occurrence of 'remember' (or the species-name) the term 'know' without changing the meaning. In other words, when someone remembers in one of these three senses, he is not "recovering the past" but showing that he knows. The basic inference to be drawn from this is that the attribution of memory in senses (1) to (3) to someone else is not a warrant for that person to make the claim 'I remember' unless he can add to what he knows the recollection of a time lapse since the last exercise of the knowledge. (This is simply a restatement of condition (3) of the necessary conditions mentioned above.) This sense, it has been suggested, is derived from the ability to recall, which cannot be described as knowing without change of meaning.

Remembering in the first three senses then is a disposition or capacity whose exercise is behavior: showing that one knows by performance or verbal behavior. Remembering in the fourth sense is an *experience* for which it does not seem adequate behavioral criteria can be stipulated.

If a computer can be said to know, then knowing and remembering would seem to coincide for it: whatever it knows it remembers and whatever it remembers it knows (it can reproduce whatever is in its memory banks). However for human beings the range of knowing and remembering overlaps, but also overflows, as it were, on either side. The following schema represents this situation:

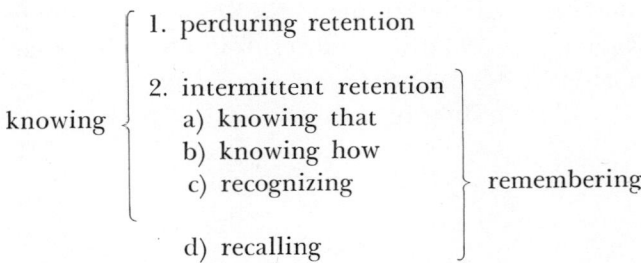

We have already seen that recall cannot be construed as knowledge. But we have also adverted to the fact that there are senses of knowing which cannot normally be construed as remembering. All of these relate to my knowledge of my personal situation in the world. Knowing my name, where I am, my wife, and so on are forms of knowledge which, as it were, are "always with me," which characterize the basic physiognomy of my familiar everyday world. It is indeed significant that any forgetting of these things is psycho-pathological in a strict sense. Moreover in this area alone is it the case that *only after* I can be said to have forgotten them can I be said to remember them. Ordinarily one may be said to have forgotten only after one did or could have remembered. Here, however, just the opposite is true.

All of these concluding remarks are tentative

and need further investigation. But they do make clear, it seems, that until conceptual clarification of this sort about remembering and forgetting is attained, the meaning of efforts to simulate these functions will be ambiguous. Knowing precisely what a given experimental result implies about the possibility of imitating human behavior requires an understanding of the behavior in question.

NOTES

1. W. Elsasser, *The Physical Foundations of Biology* (New York: Pergamon Press, 1958), p. 138.
2. R. Gerard, "What is Memory," *Scientific American*, 189, 3 (1953), 118.
3. E. Danto, "On Consciousness In Machines" in *Dimensions of Mind,* S. Hook, ed. (New York: Collier Books, 1960), p. 169; "to answer at $t + \triangle t$ a question Q asked at t is to recall Q. And I should think it follows from the fact that something is recalled by x that x is conscious." See also M. Arbib, *Brains, Machines and Mathematics* (New York: McGraw-Hill, 1964), p. 43, and J. Culbertson, *The Minds of Robots* (Urbana: University of Illinois Press, 1963), p. 381.
4. K. Sayre, *Recognition: A Study in the Philosophy of Artificial Intelligence* (Notre Dame: University of Notre Dame Press, 1965).
5. A *caveat* on the sense of the term 'image' is appropriate here. As the word is used above, it does not denote a photographic simulacrum of the experience,

a picture or sense-datum which one scans, and so on. The physical or metaphysical status of the image—for example, whether the term designates an object, whether the past "exists," and so forth—is left undecided in noting that in recalling we have the experience of doing something like attending to a given. The temptation of psychologists and philosophers has been to try to describe imagining in terms of observing.

6. J. Eccles, *Neurophysiological Basis of Mind* (Oxford: Oxford University Press, 1953).

7. W. Penfield and L. Roberts, *Speech and Brain Mechanisms* (Princeton: Princeton University Press, 1959); quoted in D. Wooldridge, *The Machinery of the Brain* (New York: McGraw-Hill, 1963), p. 167.

8. Actually after having made the distinction, little has been done by information theorists to elaborate on 'meaning.' For what follows see N. Abramson, *Information Theory and Coding* (New York: McGraw-Hill, 1963), Chap. 2.

9. *Ibid.*, p. 23.

10. D. M. McKay, "Informational Analysis of Questions and Commands" in *Information Theory: 4th London Symposium,* C. Cherry, ed., (London: Butterworth and Co., Ltd., 1961), p. 470.

11. For example, W. Bexton, W. Heron, and T. Scott, "Effects of Decreased Variation in the Sensory Environment," *Canadian Journal of Psychology,* 8 (1954), 70–76; J. Zubeck, "Behavioral and EEG Changes after 14 Days of Perceptual Deprivation," *Psychonomic Science,* 1 (1964), 57–58.

12. F. Attneave, "Some Informational Aspects of Visual Perception," *Psychological Review,* 61 (1954), 183–193; "Symmetry, Information and Memory for

Patterns," *American Journal of Psychology*, 68 (1955), 209; J. Hochberg, "Quantitative Approach to Figural Goodness," *Journal of Experimental Psychology*, 46, 5 (1953), 361.

13. J. Hochberg, *loc. cit.*

14. These figures are from a paper given by N. Hutler at the IFIP Congress in New York, May 1965. For a discussion of such an analysis of music see L. Meyer, "Meaning in Music and Information Theory," *Journal of Aesthetics and Art Criticism* (1957), 412–424.

15. For the development of this distinction see P. Geach, *Mental Acts* (London: Routledge and Kegan Paul, 1957).

16. See N. Sutherland, "Stimulus Analysing Mechanisms" in *The Modeling of Mind*, K. Sayre and F. Crosson, eds. (Notre Dame: University of Notre Dame Press, 1963).

17. For a summary of these experiments see G. Hartmann, *Gestalt Psychology* (New York: The Ronald Press Co., 1935), Chap. 9.

18. Computers, however, can be commanded to wipe out their memories. Is this forgetting?

OBEYING RULES AND FOLLOWING INSTRUCTIONS

D. B. Burrell

ONE OF THE WAYS OF COMING CLEARER IN OUR understanding of both men and machines is to trace similarities and differences in the way we use behavior expressions of both. The expressions chosen to be examined are 'following instructions' and 'obeying rules.' One might have said simply 'following instructions' and 'following rules,' but it will appear more accurate to speak of obeying rules, though this may not prove to be the case when we try to use the expressions of machines. The procedure will be to highlight those situations where instructions are given by comparing and contrasting them with typical rule-governed situations. The conceptual differences between 'following instructions' and 'obeying rules' will also come up for analysis.[1] From a clearer understanding of the uses of these expressions in human situations we can test some responsible applications to machine performance. The tack then will be to examine what rules and instructions mean to us and what different behavioral responses they elicit in an effort to discover what one might mean by asserting that computers follow instructions or obey rules.

One writer on the subject has used the two terms 'rules' and 'instructions' to define a machine: "we understand by a cybernetical machine an apparatus which performs a set of operations according to a definite set of *rules*. Normally we program a machine; that is we give it a set of *instructions* about what it is to do in each eventuality. The complete *rules* will determine the operations completely at every stage; at every stage there will be a definite *instruction* (or definite alternative instructions)."[2] Lucas compares programming with giving someone a set of instructions. His use of 'rules' here is a most radical one, not unlike Aristotle's "acting according to one's nature," for the rules to which he refers determine the operations of the machine. Hence one could not speak of obeying them, for there is no possibility of disobeying them. Since we shall be concerned with obeying rules, Lucas' use, while it does show up another sense of the term, will not be of immediate help to us.

PRELIMINARY DISTINCTIONS

It makes sense to ask someone whether he has

received his instructions, since instructions are often *given* to someone. This way of posing the question sets instructions off from *rules* on the one hand and *directions* on the other. If the more colloquial 'get' (in the sense of 'receive') is used, it simply does not make sense to ask if one has gotten the rules, but we can ask 'Did you get directions?' Although the linguistic differences are not hard and fast, there are indications that 'instructions' is the more proper term when an immediate person or an identifiable group of recipients is envisaged, while directions seem to be offered "to whom it may concern." The printed material enclosed in a model airplane package or packed with a crated piece of furniture may be entitled "Directions" or "Instructions" for assembling. At this stage there seems to be little difference. But we ask directions of a gas station attendant, not instructions. Also we feel free to waive an offer of directions when we already know the way, but we would look impertinent, certainly, if we turned down a set of instructions given or sent *to* us. For when the accent is on instructions as something given to a person or group, their origin becomes significant as well: they come *from* someone or some office *to* another person or office. But if we depart forgetting to get directions, we normally feel free to ask them of anyone else who knows the way. In summary, there seems to be a note of the juridical or imperative present when instructions are given, whereas directions are not given but merely offered. The terms, however, may be used interchangeably when this aspect is irrelevant.

The differences are more pronounced between instructions and rules, however. 'Did you get the rules?', I suggested, would make no sense at all. It would have to be interpreted as 'Did you receive a copy of them?' or by an even more idiomatic use of 'get': 'Did you understand them the way they were announced?' Rules do not need to be given to us or even offered. They simply accompany certain contexts. If we want to function in a certain situation, our activity is ipso facto subject to certain rules. Sometimes these rules are formulated, as in statutes or regulations; often they are not that explicit, as in rules of proper linguistic behavior. The fact that rules need not be formulated explicitly yet are no less normative suggests a notable difference between them and instructions where clarity is a prime desideratum. Consider, for example, the different senses of 'learn' in the admonitions 'Learn to follow instructions (or directions)!' and 'Learn to follow (or obey) rules!' The first would probably best be translated 'Attend to the message and act on it,' while the second advises a person to incorporate them into his normal conduct, to learn *how* to act in accordance with them. Rules are not made for an isolated action, since they cover habitual or recurrent activity. Instructions can be given for a single performance or for repeated performances, but whether or not the performance is repeated is strictly irrelevant. Rules, on the other hand, presuppose a background of ongoing activity, portions of which they purport to regulate.[3]

The relevance or irrelevance of background activity yields one of the most telling differences between following instructions and obeying rules. One may follow or fail to follow instructions, but with rules there is another possible attitude beyond obeying or disobeying them. We may decide that the rule is not applicable in this case. Since instructions are given precisely for an occasion, it is hard to decide they do not apply. In fact the term 'apply' is simply not used here. Hence, if I take a route other than the one prescribed and fail to make a rendezvous, I have simply failed to follow instructions—whatever my excuse may be. But with rules I may find a particular set of circumstances sufficiently unusual or a case deserving enough to warrant my deciding that the rules established are not now applicable. This possibility arises from an implicit reference to background activity. Normal and recurrent patterns of activity are presupposed in formulating any rule. Where these are sufficiently altered, one may decide the rule inapplicable. (In fact a judgment that the present set of circumstances is "sufficiently altered" from normal is but another way of describing a decision as to a rule's applicability.)

Here we have the reason why exceptions play such a privileged role in any discussion of rules. For they help to determine the range of a rule by making more explicit the typical background situations presupposed in its formulation. Hence the legal principle: *exceptio probat regulam in casibus non exceptis,* where 'probat' is translated 'proves' in the sense of testing the law's range of application and so modifying what its original meaning may have been for us. Certain exceptions may have been explicitly noted or sanctioned by custom. These would be part of the original meaning. The "cases not so exempted," however, represent those requiring a decision in practice, and these decisions help to carve out the meaning of a rule statement.

Here we have a critical difference between instructions and rules. Rules are formulated with an eye to typical situations, since their purpose is to order ongoing activity. Instructions are employed simply to prescribe certain definite performances and so can be formulated and communicated with relative unconcern about the context within which the activity is to take place. Or, to put it more positively, the procedures laid down in the instructions are so fitted to a normal set of human capacities that no alternative routes are required. Instructions (or directions) how to register to vote, how to apply for a driver's license, how to use a voting machine, as well as instructions where to lead the column of troops, how to cast one's votes as a delegate, where to unload bombs unused over target—all these are directed to people presumed to have the capacity to understand them and carry them out. Where this proves impossible, an explicit appeal can sometimes be made, and the person or office who gave the original instructions may supply an alternative set to achieve the goal intended. But there is no middle ground between following or not following an instruction. A delegate may decide to vote in a way which would actually prove closer to the desires of his constituents than the slate for which they directed him to vote, but he would not be following instructions in so acting.

Because instructions relate to a particular end and specify the way to reach that end, there is no leeway to act in accordance with them while one proceeds at variance with any one of the specified procedures. Nor is this a "rigid" interpretation of instructions; it is simply a matter of the logic of the term. There could be an understanding between instructor and instructed that one may adopt alternative courses of action at variance with the explicit program when one deems it reasonable. But whoever did so could be asked to explain why he had failed to follow instructions. Can we consider such an understanding a further instruction or add it as a rider to a set of instructions? It seems not, for recommending that someone act reasonably does not tell him what to do or supply directions how to act. It may have to be made explicit to some, or in certain cases explicitly suppressed—as when a specially coordinated set of activities demands a literal adherence of all involved—but counsels such as these refer to the manner in which one treats instructions. Instructions however are given to be followed. Normal human canons of reasonable behavior may be invoked to explain why someone failed to follow his instructions, but the fact remains that someone did fail to follow them.

This suggests certain intrinsic limitations on the usefulness of instructions, limitations imposed by a role which requires a definite goal and a specific route to it. Where the activity is self-contained and does not carry over into widening contexts, one can learn how to perform it simply by following instructions. Operating a voting machine or a record changer would be good examples. But one cannot teach someone how to drive a car with a set of instructions. Here the tools of instruction seem rather to be rules of behavior for typical situations. When we teach another how to drive, there are certain initial and terminal instructions, to be sure, but the process of controlling the vehicle in traffic is governed by sets of rules. For one is not merely concerned with getting from here to there or with executing a sequence of actions, but with learning how to execute a patterned activity in an ever-widening context. If it were simply a case of recurrent but self-contained activity, instructions would suffice to inculcate the habit, but where the activity itself will require to be "integrated" with many other activities and meet eventualities too numerous to be foreseen, we require a different kind of generality—that of rules.[4]

GENERALITY OF RULES

The generality of rules, as we have noted already, must be compatible with exceptions, cases in which one judges the rule inapplicable. In works on ethics these are often referred to as "deserving" cases.[5] The judgment itself cannot be rule-governed, since the question of applicability would arise again with the governing rule. Does "No Motor Vehicles Allowed in the Park" exclude the ambulance, the paraplegic's electric cart, the motorized model airplane, the Good Humor man? To be effective in regulating a situation, the rule must cover every case in question. A case is "deserving," not because it is unlikely or statistically irrelevant, but rather when it is seen or judged not to be one of those in question, even though it is literally a candidate.

How are these judgments made? How does one learn the proper generality of rules? The response of the common law tradition has been to list typical cases covered by the law and consider reasons offered why certain others are sufficiently different not to be. Decisions rendered on these contested cases help determine the meaning of the statute. The style of argument is designed to show that the order the law "intends" would be ill-served by following out the letter in this case. By familiarizing himself with this kind of appeal one learns the kind of universality he can expect from laws. (Casuistry in ethics can serve a similar purpose. Its pejorative connotations of "hairsplitting" resulted from a legalistic use which appealed not to the order intended but more narrowly to other laws or loopholes. At its best casuistry is the consideration of cases in an effort to develop one's sense for the typical and for the deserving exception.)

Judgment seems to be a component of obeying rules in a way in which it does not enter into following instructions. One may be pressed to decide whether it is reasonable to follow a set of instructions, but this is a judgment *about* following them, not one involved in following them. Hence we have insisted that one either follows or fails to follow instructions, while obeying rules admits of a third course: deciding the rule inapplicable in this case.

This difference is reflected in the way the purpose of rules contrasts with the goal of instructions. A set of instructions is good if one can follow it to the end and thereby arrive at his goal, accomplish his mission, or simply execute the desired performance. The goal of a set of instructions, then, can be identified, as in a destination to be reached, a result produced, or merely the faithful execution of the instructions themselves. But rules are established to order activity presently occurring or anticipated. Yet *order* cannot be identified so clearly that one is sure he has arrived at it. Hence "good order" cannot provide a critierion for determining whether a rule is adequate or not, since we cannot give it a formulation determinate enough to make it a criterion.

The fact that "good order" resists precise formulation does not however preclude our having recourse to it in deciding whether a rule be applicable or not in this case. It is merely that rules are related to their purpose in a manner quite different from that linking instructions with their goal. Indeed the fact that we *appeal to* "good order" to justify a rule or establish a case as deserving of exception seems to be related to the "slippage" between rules and their stated purpose. The purpose is normative in a way that the goal of a set of instructions is not. One may give instructions simply by giving the goal and leaving the route to the recipient, but in this case the goal must be specifiable independently of any particular route. When the goal is not previously specified, then the instructions themselves will do so—in the operative sense that by faithfully executing them to the end we will accomplish or arrive at the goal.[6]

APPLYING THE DISTINCTION TO MACHINE ACTIVITY

If one is guided by the limited linguistic and conceptual differences we have noted, it would seem more appropriate to compare a machine program with a set of instructions than with rules. Where the program is "debugged," the machine may execute or fail to execute it, but cannot decide it inapplicable. (The process of "debugging" involves removing any ambiguous formulations or references and adhering to the rules of the programming language so as to mesh with the capabilities of the machine. Instructions must be clear and tailored to the capacities of the recipient.) And a program, like instructions, is not strictly speaking applicable or inapplicable. It is given as something to be carried out. It would be awkward to speak of "acting in accordance with a program" (or a set of instructions), while it is quite natural to refer to one's acting in accordance with rules. We should rather speak of following a program in the sense of executing it.

Some programs may prove useful time and again, and be stored as permanent components of the machine available for repeated use. The supplied functions and available subroutines are examples of these. But even though they may be employed again and again, it would be inappropriate to compare these with skills of the developing variety such as knowing how to drive a car or to do mathematics. We noted that skills such as these must equip a person to function in ever-widening contexts and are most effectively learned through strategic rules and a gradual growth in judgment. To speak of the use of rules and need of judgment rather than relying on a set of instructions is a way of remarking the kind of adaptability these skills enjoy. The programmed capacities of a computer, on the other hand, are useful precisely because we know exactly what they will do. They are rather more like those circumscribed behavior patterns that we have learned via instructions, that we can count on and must revise only in the face of failure—such as operating ordinary appliances, unlocking and opening doors, turning off the ignition and putting the keys in one's pocket. The very utility of a function subroutine—the fact that we know precisely what it can do—leaves no question how to apply it. The only question is whether or not to call it in this situation.[7]

In executing a program a computer could better be said to be following instructions than obeying rules. The process wherein one takes pains to formulate the instructions in an appropriate language and delivers the deck to an operator constitutes the activity of handing instructions *to* the computer. The context is established by the listed capacity of the machine and the uses to which we intend to put it.

Can it ever be said that a computer obeys rules? So far we have located a salient difference between following instructions and obeying rules in the judgment of applicability. While instructions permit of no other response than following or not, rules may be obeyed, disobeyed, or judged inapplicable. We observed a sense of 'rule' used by Lucas —the rules determining a machine's operation— which is not germane. The machine cannot be said to "obey" them since it cannot disobey them. However there remain myriad senses of 'rule,' some of which we shall have to isolate in order to pose this question more accurately.

BASIC DIVISIONS WITHIN RULES

So far we have been speaking of rules in the familiar sense of regulations. We might designate these as institutional rules opening out towards laws, as institutions open towards society. There are of course other kinds of rules. Two other types of rule seem important to our considerations: rules of logical procedure and rules of a game. Rules of either sort operate in a context far more confined than institutional rules. Indeed part of the function of rules both in logic and in games is to define or constitute a context—a "universe of discourse" or a field of play. By rules of logical procedure is meant authorizations like *Modus ponens*. This can be read: "when we are entitled to lay down something of the shape Cpq and also entitled to lay down something of the shape p, we are further entitled to lay down something of the shape q." In the context the sorts of things we are entitled to "lay down" are either stipulated or constructed unambiguously by other rules.

This gives logical rules a peculiar status. No rule can succeed in stating how it is to be applied.[8] For this would require another rule statement, and there would always be question as to how *it* should be applied. In law an entire discipline has developed around the myriad applications and interpretations of a statute. In each person's more humble encounters with rules a growing sensitivity and judgment guides him toward a sensible respect which steers between rigidity and laxity. But logical rules have a privileged status. The activity they are fashioned to regulate is already circumscribed by other rules in such a way that the rules of logic *show* how they are to be applied even if they cannot *state* it. The complexus of rules together with the symbolic alphabet defines a "system" so well that any single rule leaves no question as to its application. Logical rules, algorithms, and recursive functions are all of this type; there is no doubt as to their application.[9] The use of different type face in proposing the rule is intended to *show* that it functions as a rule; its being cast in a metalanguage reveals its role of regulating possible movements and combinations which can be carried out with the logical alphabet.

Since the major delineation between rules and instructions has been drawn at the judgment of applicability, it is hard to see how rules of logic could qualify as rules. Should we say they are a kind of second-level instruction: "Whenever something of such a shape appears, DO such and such"? Since they do not tell us what to do, but what we are entitled to do, there is reason for calling them rules. They do not themselves provide a goal or aim for what one might do with a logical system. That is more a question of the logician's purpose and is implemented by various "strategies." Since they inform us of what can be done, and not of what we are to do, they seem better candidates for rules than instructions. C. S. Peirce suggests that the most generic possible sense of 'rule' is "a general formula applicable to particular cases."[10] This would allow us to speak of logical rules of procedure as rules in a reductive or minimal sense, even though the more interesting questions of application never arise. It is clear that computers can and do follow this sort of rule, though neither a computer nor a logician could be said to *obey* them.

One might question my refusing these rules full-fledged status by proposing them as the clearest possible example of a rule, namely, one whose application leaves nothing to doubt. In responding to this objection we will unearth a radical difference between these rules and other kinds, one which explains why they seem to be able to *show* their own application.

We normally meet rules laid down to regulate ongoing activity, usually by prohibiting certain forms of it (parietal rules) or prescribing that definite priorities or procedures be adhered to where certain types of activity are deemed especially in need of regulation (examination rubrics). It is presupposed that activity is already going on, and the rules are intended to regulate this activity rather than to exclude all procedures except those specifically designated. And where rules are imposed upon a background of ongoing activity without attempting to legislate any and all acceptable forms of activity, questions of applicability are bound to arise. For the number of combinations is endless and the very combinations which can be said to constitute this activity are not well defined. Hence to prescribe all permissible forms of activity would be a practical and a theoretic impossibility. One must content himself with proscribing certain kinds and prescribing procedural patterns in certain privileged cases.

But since one cannot always be clear whether the activity he meets is in fact of the type proscribed —or whether in this set of circumstances it is even subject to the proscription—rules of this kind need to be administered. The administrator or judge is faced with a double judgment: (1) that this bit of activity is indeed of the type proscribed (or required) and (2) that the entire situation is sufficiently typical so as to fall under the rule. (In the face of a general rule to keep to one's own lane in freeway driving one may still ask whether a driver who is skilled and careful while somewhat prone to shift to more advantageous lanes when the opportunity offers itself is in fact "changing lanes too often" and hence "driving recklessly." Or we may admit that a particular driver was indeed shifting lanes far too often but find the circumstances sufficiently unusual to warrant it—say, an emergency run to the hospital). By contrast, however, rules of logic might be said to "administer themselves." In this sense they can be said to *show* their own application.

The affinities between 'rule,' 'regulate,' and 'administrate' suggest that rules of conduct are more representative of rules than those of logic. But the question of locating privileged uses of an analogous term like 'rules' is presently more a strategic than a philosophic one. It will suffice for now to have identified an important difference between rules of conduct and rules of a calculus according as the rule in some way gives its own application or needs to be administered. But the deeper difference which allows one to contrive the situation in which a rule can show its own application seems to be the relevance or irrelevance of ongoing background activity. Rules as we ordinarily meet them are established to order such activity; rules of a calculus are supposed to legislate any and every move and combination of objects which will be countenanced. The first kind aim at ordering an environment within a larger world; the latter at establishing a world itself, a "universe of discourse."

GAME RULES

Games provide us with another example of rules which would constitute a context as well as regulate activity within it. In this they are quite similar to those of logic, though they are a more familiar part of our life and so should supply more interest and variations than rules of logical procedure. Our ordinary parlance also links rules with games quite closely, so that game playing gives a certain coloration to the notion of *rule*.

As with logical rules, we cannot disobey game rules. We simply cannot play a game and at the same time not play according to the rules.[11] To play a game entails abiding by certain rules; these are not two separate activities: to play and to play according to the rules. And if playing a game means keeping certain rules, cheating is only pretending to play the game. (We are referring here exclusively to those rules which constitute the available or legal moves in the game. There are other rules, "rules of thumb," which are recommendations about how to proceed. These are better called "strategies," for they are empirically developed and carry no sanctions [except perhaps defeat] for not following them.)

Game rules are again similar to logical rules in establishing permitted moves, in legislating what is to count as a move. (We have summarized this function as "constituting a context.") They also proscribe certain behavior, of course, but it seems that this function is subservient to the first. The proscriptions attempt to cope with eventualities arising from the newly created matrix of activities by settling conflict situations and clarifying ambiguities which may arise. Questions of application which do arise are settled as they arise by formulating new rules. However there may remain some doubt whether the moves made or contemplated are clearly of a certain type. Here one can distinguish rather easily those games which need a referee and those which do not. Active sports, for example, count on a good deal of activity and many capabilities which have to be ordered to the end of the game. It is not always easy to determine whether a certain type is "in bounds." Games like chess and checkers, however, require a minimum of dexterity, so that the moves can be clearly, even abstractly, defined, which makes a referee superfluous.

The referee's task however is limited to deciding

whether or not the action performed was of a type permitted (or proscribed). He cannot decide that the rule is not applicable in this case. At least he cannot decide so without stepping out of his role as referee, as when an accident occurs which "breaks up the game." So while some games admit a kind of decision of applicability analogous to deciding whether someone's manner of driving is actually "reckless," there is no room for the full decision, namely, that such driving might well be countenanced in this unusual case. For once one decides to play a game, he submits by that very fact to its rules. In return for this self-limitation however he gains certain immunities: a hard tackle on the field is part of the game, whereas it could be considered assault on the street.

Considering this difference between creating a context (rules of logical procedure and games) and regulating activity within an open context has led at least one author to divide rules into two basic types: *constitutive* and *regulative*.[12] Constitutive rules will also regulate but will do so in the manner described above for logic or games. That is, there may be questions about an action being one of those proscribed but never any question about applying the law itself.

What about machines? What sort of games can they play? It seems that they could be programmed to play any game which needs no referee, where the possible moves are clearly defined and abstractly executable—not calling for muscular prowess, finesse, and the like. In playing such a game the computer will be following rules but doing so in a fashion similar to those of logic. No questions of applicability will arise. Preferential strategies will be required of course, for in playing a game we are not so much taken up with rules as bounded by them. The strategies occupy our attention and are in many ways more interesting than the rules. But these are empirically derived and not immediately germane to the present discussion.

If a machine can play a game, can it also cheat at it? It does not seem that it could. For if we overlook the intentional connotations of 'cheating,' it remains that "teaching the machine to play a game" means providing it with strategies developed in accordance with the rules. Insofar as other strategies might be employed they would not have been developed in conjunction with this game and hence would not constitute "playing this particular game." The machine of course could end up employing another set of strategies in any particular instance due to electronic failures, but that would not qualify as "cheating." Nor of course are we entitled to call the machine "honest," for one who *cannot* cheat is neither honest nor dishonest.

FURTHER AND UNRESOLVED QUESTIONS

Rules play a prominent part in games but in a manner which makes their presence incontestable. It is perhaps this quite hospitable fit of rules with game situations which gives to game rules a certain linguistic priority. For "those are the rules of the game" is often heard and invoked when regulations and not game rules are at stake, as though assimilating the situation to a game would make following the rules more palatable. Game rules are uniquely ordered to the goal of the game, however that might be described, and tempered by concerns for aesthetics and simplicity. So long as ordinary mores are respected, the rules are not contestable except in relation to the goal of the game itself, so no question of their reasonableness arises.

The net effect of such total subservience to a goal is what one might call a pseudo enterprise. Games have a point which itself has no point. Games do not go anywhere, and this leads some people to find them unreasonable *in toto*. Yet their role in human life, their significance, if you will, as a human endeavor, seems to rest heavily on this very fact that they do *not* "go anywhere," that their point is sufficiently self-contained to be pointless in any broader context. And all this seems to make rules more palatable within a game environment. Once we have accepted the desirability of relating our actions so unilaterally or centripetally to a goal, it is only reasonable that rules be laid down to make it operate more smoothly. There is an obvious value to rules in a game situation.

We invite a person not to take censure or failure personally by reminding him "those are the rules of the game"; a person in authority invites respect for a set of regulations that governs his own activities as well as those to whom he is speaking by suggesting "play fair with me and I'll play fair with you." A professional soldier comes to view war as a game and is often quite scrupulous about proper ways of waging it, as if to demonstrate how one can take something quite inhuman and irrational and succeed in directing his attention to what is ordered and reasonable about it. The model best adapted to this transfer seems to be the game.

Once our attention is drawn to these points, it seems that 'rule' fits games more closely than either calculus or conduct. We have already noted that its use in a calculus was quite specialized and restrictive. On the other hand, 'rule' seems itself too restrictive a term to apply to the regulation of conduct. There is something demeaning, hard, and unyielding about the phrase 'rule-governed conduct.' We normally feel much more comfortable with the metaphorical expression 'guidelines,' which connotes a background of ongoing activity, a kind of journey rather than an isolated goal. One senses that 'rules' fit but clumsily with the flexibility, respect for diversity, and open texture of human activity, at least as we would like to see it governed.

INSTITUTIONAL RULES

This linguistic malaise about 'rules of conduct' also signals the limits of fruitful questions about computers following rules. Beyond the rules of logic and games the area of institutional rules opens out so widely and with such diversity as to be clearly outside the ken of this limited discussion. Furthermore the connotations surrounding 'regulations,' 'laws,' 'customs,' and 'conventions' are so richly human that to ask whether a computer could follow them would be closer to science fiction than analysis.

Yet it is rules of this sort that we speak of obeying, disobeying, or judging inapplicable. One does not obey logical rules but simply follows them. Not to follow the rules of a game is cheating, not disobedience. Furthermore, since institutional rules normally presuppose and regulate activity of a certain variety without pretending to constitute it *as* activity of that kind, one continues to drive even if he does so in a fashion contrary to the traffic rules in force. To cheat *at* bridge however is to cease for the moment to play the game, since the rules only countenance certain moves as bridge moves. (The fact that cheating is sometimes a physical possibility does not mean it must be a logical one as well. The discrepancy lies with the activity presupposed in making the constituted moves. Where the moves are abstractly defined and executed, the physically and logically possible merge, for the margin of dissimulation vanishes.)

It makes little or no sense then to ask whether computers obey rules in the full sense, which involves a possible judgment of applicability. The language in which we describe such a judgment seems clearly foreign to that which has been seen apropos of machine behavior. For what I have called a "judgment of applicability" involves locating the relevant factors in the situation at hand and weighing them against those normally considered relevant to determine whether a rule can be invoked at face value. We speak of it as a judgment rather than a calculation, since relevance involves an appraisal of sorts and has always eluded the kind of formulation that would make it amenable to calculation. The recurring reference to a normal "background" represents another attempt to point up the need for a judgment. For one recognizes a background by its *salient* features, and while we might conceivably program a computer with those features we have recognized to be salient, the further process of weighing different features against these to decide whether the case at hand be *sufficiently* different to warrant its deserving special attention seems quite beyond the formal capacities of machine comparison. For the weighing and the decision about a sufficient difference involve appealing to values like "good order." And though we regularly appeal to values like these in making such judgments, we do not invoke them as formal criteria because they are not susceptible of so precise a formulation.

Linguistic differences such as these, as thoroughgoing and exclusive as they may be, cannot close off further inquiry. It *could* be that judgments like those described, if understood in all their components, would best be explained as made up of simpler procedures more amenable to computer simulation. Then if the "make-up" itself were similarly explicable, a new and explanatory understanding would result which should lead to new descriptive categories for our language. But the present and pervasive linguistic differences *do* have possession, and proposals to suppress them will have to be based on research rather than recommendation.

Computers can function as models which illuminate by contrast as well as by similarity. In this spirit we have shown how one can fruitfully compare programs with instructions, in what senses computers can be said to follow rules and in what senses not. In every case, whether the "fit" was apt or not, the use of this model provided a new kind of illumination for the areas of human behavior in question.

NOTES

1. I am especially indebted to Professors Frederick Crosson and Kenneth Sayre for suggestions about the conceptual distinctions elaborated here at the outset, results of discussions at Notre Dame in the summer of 1965.

2. J. Lucas, "Minds, Machines and Gödel" in *The Modeling of Mind: Computers and Intelligence*, K.

Sayre and F. Crosson, eds. (Notre Dame: University of Notre Dame Press, 1963), pp. 256–257.

3. Two communications to the faculty at the University of Notre Dame from the Academic Affairs Office illustrate this difference quite clearly: one, entitled "Counselling and Advance Registration Instructions," lists five consecutive steps for students to take in order to preregister. Each step has two or more subheads, all referring to procedures to be followed in order. The other, "Final Examination Regulations," contains six entries which are not consecutive but cover standard eventualities and set up procedures to be followed or sanctions to be invoked. Within this format many instructions occur, of course, but the over-all orientation is designed to gear the scheduling and administering of exams into some of the typical eventualities of student and academic life. The prior communication prescinds entirely from ongoing activity and simply lists steps to be taken in the order they should be taken.

4. Gilbert Ryle documents this difference as one between *habits* and *intelligent capacities*: "We build up habits by drill but we build up intelligent capacities by training. . . . Training, . . . though it embodies plenty of sheer drill, does not consist of drill. It involves the simulation of criticism and example of the pupil's own judgment. He learns how to do things thinking what he is doing so that every operation performed is itself a new lesson to him how to perform better." (*Concept of Mind* [New York: Barnes and Noble, 1949], pp. 42–43).

5. See K. Baier, *The Moral Point of View,* abridged ed. (New York: Random House, 1965), pp. 96–100. This section on the generality of general moral precepts is especially recommended.

6. To distinguish between *goal* and *purpose* may sound gratuitous, but it receives support both from ordinary usage and the literature on "goal-directed" automata. To note a distinction between uses does not say that the terms will always be used differently. The language of intent is notoriously rich and overlapping. Yet we speak of a destination as the goal of a trip where we could never claim arriving at a certain place as our purpose in undertaking the trip. In this sense the goal of a mission can be identified with its end result, while its purpose is more directly linked with the intent for which it was carried out. "Where are you going?" "What are you planning to do?" can be answered by supplying the goal; "Why are you doing that?" asks for the purpose.

Talk about goals then, especially when it is linked with following a set of instructions to the finish, can be carried out in terms devoid of intent, while attempts to coin explicitly nonintentional cognates of 'purpose' —like 'purposive'—always seem suspect. (See the discussion between Richard Taylor, Norbert Wiener, and Arturo Rosenblueth, *Philosophy of Science,* 17 (1950), 310–332.)

Writers on machine activity speak of goals and goal-directed activity in terms more akin to instructions than rules. Donald MacKay asserts that goal-directed activity is easily mechanically simulated where the pattern is a function of unique and precisely definable reactions to precisely definable situations—in other words, where one can instruct what to do in which eventualities ("Mindlike Behaviour in Artifacts," *British Journal for the Philosophy of Science,* 2 (1951–1952), 228–229). J. Licklider prefers to distinguish between goals (for men) and a course of action (for machines) where the latter entails specifying the course to be taken stepwise and sequentially—after the fashion of a set of instructions ("Man-Computer Symbiosis," *IRE Transactions on Human Factors in Electronics,* HFE–1 (March 1960), 4–11).

7. With some ingenuity subroutines of this ordinary sort can be linked together in a manner which simulates some limited forms of adaptability. The result is a program capable of correcting its deviations and designed to adopt those tactical moves which prove more conducive to accomplishing the designated goal. In this sense they are "self-adaptive." Whether correcting deviations can be termed "learning by its mistakes" or whether adopting tactics which prove to be oriented more clearly to a definite goal is properly called "learning by experience" remains an obscure question so long as terms like 'learning' are so contested. It is clear however that to speak of "growing" or generating "subroutines of organizing activity which will have developed through adaptive success" is metaphorical in the extreme.

8. The classic statement, often reprinted, is that of Lewis Carroll, "What the Tortoise Said to Achilles," *Mind,* N.S. IV, 14 (1895), 278–280.

9. There are of course many doubts as soon as one raises his epistemological sights beyond the context within which logicians are accustomed to work. But so long as one remains therein, things work in the uncomplicated fashion sketched here. This is the enduring part of Wittgenstein's distinction in the *Tractatus* between *saying* and *showing,* which has obviously guided the thinking here. His later and serious reservations, especially those in *Remarks on the Foundations of Mathematics,* threaten the comfortable isolation of the

Tractarian doctrine, but not its truth in isolation.

10. C. S. Peirce, *Collected Papers* (Cambridge, Mass.: Harvard University Press, 1931) 1.606. Peirce defines an algebraic rule as "a permission under strictly defined conditions" (4.361) and then appends the following remarks in note 1: "This curious use of the word 'rule' is doubtless derived from the use of the word in vulgar arithmetic, where it signifies a method of computation adapted to a particular class of problems. . . . Here the rule is a body of directions for performing an operation successfully. But when we speak of the rule of transposition, the directions are so simple that the rule becomes principally a permission."

11. Anthony Ralls, "Game of Life," *Philosophical Quarterly*, 16 (1966), 23–34.

12. J. Searle, "How to Derive 'Ought' from 'Is'" *Philosophical Review*, 73 (1964), 55; relying on J. Rawls, "Two Concepts of Rules," *Philosophical Review*, 64 (1955), 3–32.

INSTRUMENTATION AND MECHANICAL AGENCY

K. M. Sayre

1. IT IS COMMONPLACE THAT PEOPLE USE machines as instruments. Equally apparent, it might be thought, is that machines can be used only as instruments and that they themselves are not capable of using instruments in turn. If this were so, it would indicate a basic difference between the agency of machines and the agency of human beings.

I want to argue against this particular distinction between human and mechanical agency. In preparation it will be necessary to distinguish generally between instrumental and noninstrumental acts, after which it may be considered whether machines are limited to one sort alone. That machines are capable of acts of *some* sort I consider unproblematical for reasons to appear later. Let us turn to an analysis of the concept of instrumentation.

2. There is a distinction between statements of agency regarding which the question 'what with?' makes sense and those regarding which it does not. For example, if it is said that a stone (perhaps thrown by a boy playing outside) or a nut (perhaps dislodged from the tree above) broke the window of John's greenhouse, it would be senseless to ask in return what the stone or the nut broke the window with. But if it is said that the boy playing outside broke John's window, it would be sensible and conceivably quite pertinent to inquire what he broke the window with. Whether and in what fashion John decides to pursue the matter might depend upon the answer to this question.

Now when the question 'what with?' is appropriately asked regarding an action, the event of that action's performance may be reported appropriately in an expression of the form 'X did-A with Y' (or simply 'X A'd with Y'). When this question is not pertinent, the performance of the action is reported appropriately in an expression of the form 'X did-A' (or simply 'X A'd'). Typical of the former are 'the boy broke the window with the stone' and 'John chased the boy with his walking stick.' Typical of the latter are 'the stone broke the window' and 'John cursed.'

When it is appropriate to say that X did-A with Y, it is not necessarily inappropriate thereby to say as well regarding the same act that A was done by Y. Thus, for example, we might say with equal propriety either that the bird dislodged the nut with its wing or that the bird's wing dislodged the nut. In like fashion we might say equally well that the oak tree hove up the nearby sidewalk with its roots or that the roots of the tree hove up the sidewalk. And if John, running outside to see what had happened, is tripped unintentionally in his wife's knitting, it would seem equally fitting to say either that she had tripped him in her yarn or that his wife's yarn had tripped John as he was running by the place she was sitting.

3. There is a further distinction between statements of agency which can be formulated appropriately under either format and those for which the format 'X did-A with Y' is appropriate but for which the format 'Y did-A' would be either wrong or misleading. The former are illustrated by the examples above. The latter may be illustrated by supposing a situation in which the window was intentionally broken by the boy. If it is the case that the stone which broke the window was thrown intentionally, it would be misleading to say merely that the stone broke the window. In response to the question "Who, or what, broke the window?", the reply "The stone did it" has obvious shortcomings in comparison with the more complete reply "The boy broke the window with the stone." To say that the stone broke the window conveys different information from the report that the boy

broke the window with the stone, and it might be a matter of importance to determine which is the more appropriate thing to say.

We shall consider one verbal expression to be more appropriate than another in the description of a given situation if the former contains information about the situation (1) which the other lacks and (2) the omission of which would lead one to form a misleading or otherwise inadequate conception of what had happened in the situation on the basis of this description alone.

4. Acts which could be reported equally well under the format 'X did-A with Y' and under the format 'Y did-A' correspond generally to acts accomplished without intention. Thus in the examples above there is no intention on the part of the tree to damage the sidewalk and no intention on the part of the bird to dislodge the nut. Further, the condition which makes the case of John's wife's yarn a proper illustration is that the wife did not intend to trip John with the yarn. And if in repairing a window John unintentionally strikes his thumb with his hammer, we could say without misdescribing the situation either that John hit his thumb with the hammer or that the hammer struck John's thumb while he was repairing the window.

It is also noteworthy that things which are scarcely ever done without intention are acts which are not alternatively describable in the form 'X did-A with Y' and in the form 'Y did-A.' Since

John does not pot except when he intends to pot, although he pots with his potting tool, we would scarcely say that it is John's potting tool which does the potting. And since a slap is not a slap unless it is intentional, it would never be appropriate to say that one's hand slapped another's face, although it is appropriate often enough to say that one slapped another's face with one's hand.

Moreover, there are cases of uncertainty whether an expression of the form 'X did-A with Y' or one of the form 'Y did-A' is called for in describing an act, and in which the uncertainty could be resolved by determining whether the act was intentionally pursued. Thus if John's wife, passing through his potting shed, knocks over a pile of pots in a sweeping motion of her hand, one would be inclined to say that her hand had brushed against and knocked over the pile of pots if the act appeared unintentional, whereas one would be inclined to say that the wife had knocked over the pots with her hand if the act appeared intentional. In a similar vein it is interesting to conjecture that the reason we would hesitate to accept 'the dog's mouth picked up the shoe' as an alternative to 'the dog picked up the shoe with his mouth' but do not hesitate to accept either 'the tree's roots hove up the sidewalk' or 'the tree hove up the sidewalk with its roots' is that we tend to think that dogs, but not trees, are capable of conscious purpose and hence (in some sense) are capable of intentional action.

For all this, however, the distinction between acts which do and those which do not admit alternative descriptions in the forms 'X did-A with Y' and 'Y did-A' is *not* the same as the distinction between nonintentional and intentional acts. For there are some nonintentional acts which do not admit alternative descriptions of this sort, and there are other acts which admit such alternative descriptions but which are surely intentional. As an example of the first, consider that we would not say that John's comb arranged his hair, even if we knew that this particular activity of John's was a nervous habit, hence unconscious and unintentional. And second, if John's cane, thrown toward the boy in an effort to strike him, hits instead the roof of a nearby house and thereupon glances off to hit the boy as he rounds a corner, it would seem equally fitting to say either that John succeeded in hitting the boy with his cane or that the cane, which John threw, after a bounce or two hit the boy.

That the distinction we are considering is not that between intentional and nonintentional acts is even more evident when we consider that there are some things one might do either intentionally or otherwise which are not describable in the form 'X did-A with Y.' Although one might unintentionally fall off a cliff, for example, as against hurling oneself off purposefully, it would not make sense to say that one fell over a cliff with something or other. One drives nails with ham-

INSTRUMENTATION AND MECHANICAL AGENCY 239

mers and slaps with one's hands, but in the relevant sense one does not fall (or hurl oneself) with anything.

Let us employ these distinctions in an attempt to establish the conditions which must be met if an action is to be described correctly as having been performed with an instrument.

5. One condition which clearly is necessary for saying correctly that X used Y as an instrument in doing A is that, when asked what happened in the performance of the action in question, we should be able to respond fittingly by saying that X did-A *with* Y. Thus, although it might be appropriate on occasion to say that the stone broke the window, it would never be appropriate to say that the stone broke the window with anything, and hence it would never be appropriate to say that the stone used an instrument to break the window. Let us express this dependency as condition (1):

> (1) In response to the question "What happened?" it is correct to say 'X used Y as an instrument in doing A' only if it is appropriate to say 'X did-A with Y.'

The expression 'with Y' here must be one which cannot be replaced by a patently adverbial phrase. Thus 'John chased the boy with vigor' fails to qualify, since it could as well be expressed as 'John chased the boy vigorously.' Other expressions ruled out on this basis are 'with tears in his eyes,' 'with pleasure,' and 'with hopes of success.' On the other

sions, surely it would be foolish to say that a loud report was an instrument of the stone in breaking the window, that John's cry of dismay was an instrument in his pursuit of the culprit, or that the boy used the frightened look in his eyes as an instrument of apology. Yet since it is inappropiate to say either that the report broke the window, that the cry of dismay pursued the culprit, or that the frightened look apologized, each of these expressions meets the conditions set down in (1) and (2). So (1) and (2) together are not sufficient to clarify the conditions under which it is appropriate to say that an agent used an instrument in the accomplishment of a particular act.

It is clear what is wrong with the expressions above, but it is not clear at first how they ought to be excluded. What is wrong is that the term 'with' is used in a sense quite extraneous to the sense in which we say that something is done with an instrument. But since our task is to analyze the concept of instrument and these cases must be excluded as part of the analysis, they cannot be excluded on this ground alone.

Now the one feature which appears in common among these examples is that in each case the result, attitude, or manifestation which accompanies the act is unique to that particular act itself. In this sense, for example, the loud report which accompanied this particular act of the stone arose as a part of the over-all situation in which the act occurred and as such could not have been associated with any other activity of the same (or of any different) agent. If the stone had broken another window, there might have resulted another loud report, and there are other things the stone might do or might have done which would also result in loud noises. But this particular loud report could not accompany any other act, since it is the result of this act uniquely. Similarly, although John might cry out in dismay on many occasions and the boy's eyes might display a frightened look under many circumstances, *that* cry of dismay and *that* frightened look are associated with those acts uniquely. On the other hand, whenever we would say that the boy broke the window with the stone, we certainly would allow that other things could have been done with that particular stone, and we would not be surprised to hear of other things yet to be done with it. And no matter when John potted the geraniums with the trowel or was tripped with the ball of yarn, surely we would admit that other things could have been done with either object. With this in view let us set a third necessary condition:

> (3) In response to the question "What happened?" it is correct to say 'X used Y to A' only if there is some act B different from A such that it would be true under some conceivable circumstances to say 'X did-B with Y.'

The effect of this condition is to exclude from instrumentality those things whose accompaniment of A might be reported with the term 'with' but which for some reason or another can accompany

A alone. Just as we would say that a man does not use his stomach as an instrument for the digestion of food, since there is nothing else normally which he could do with that organ, so in general a thing which can accompany one particular act alone therefore cannot be said to be an instrument for the accomplishment of that act.

Finally we have to exclude such obvious cases as 'John walked down the path with his friend.' Although this expression meets all the criteria thus far stated, clearly we would not say that John used his friend to walk down the path. Other cases to be excluded with this are 'John purchased the fence with his neighbor,' 'John came home with his wife,' and 'John threw out the flowers with the flower pots.' The intention behind such expressions normally would be to express concomitance, a sign of which is that the meaning of the expression is preserved when the term 'with' is replaced by 'together with.' Thus we could say with equal propriety either that John walked down the path with his friend or that John walked down the path together with his friend. Similarly we might say with equal truth, if not equal parsimony of expression, that John purchased the fence together with his neighbor, that John came home together with his wife, and that John threw out the flowers together with the flower pot. Condition (4) thus may be expressed as follows:

(4) In response to the question "What happened?" it is correct to say 'X used Y as an in-

strument in doing A' only if it would not be appropriate to say 'X did-A together with Y.'

The rationale here is similar to that of condition (2): if in some straightforward sense it is correct to attribute A to Y as well as to X (as in 'John purchased the fence with his neighbor') or to include Y among the objects of the act (as in 'John threw out the flowers with the flower pot'), then it is not correct to consider Y an instrument in the accomplishment of the act.

Combining these conditions into one, we have the following complex necessary condition for the attribution of instrumentality:

(5) In response to the question "What happened?" it is correct to say 'X used Y as an instrument in doing A' only if (i) it is appropriate to say 'X did-A with Y,' (ii) it is not appropriate to say merely 'Y did-A,' (iii) there is a B different from A such that it would be true under some conceivable circumstances to say 'X did-B with Y,' and (iv) it is not appropriate to say 'X did-A together with Y.'

Since we are concerned below to determine whether any necessary conditions for instrumentality are violated in speaking of the use of instruments in the agency of machines, it is pertinent to hope that (5) is essentially complete. Before turning to problems of mechanical agency however, let us consider various human acts that are and others that are not accomplished through instrumentation.

6. It is clear that there are some human acts which on one occasion might be accomplished with an instrument and which on another might be accomplished without. Thus we would ordinarily take it that John's wife used an instrument in tripping John with her yarn if the act was intentional, but she did not use an instrument otherwise. And if John does a sum on an adding machine, we would be led by (5) to say that he used the machine for that purpose; but if John did the sum "in his head," we would not say he used his head (or his brain, or his mind) as an instrument, since we would not say that John calculated *with* his head (or with his brain, or with his mind).

There are other human acts which appear always to be accomplished with instruments. One is able to pound nails only insofar as one uses a hammer or some other instrument to do the job. If it was to be questioned on a particular occasion what John had used to pound in a particular nail, there would always be an answer if John in fact had done the pounding. Similarly one can sign his name only by using a pen, pencil, stick, or other instrument; and John is able to put dirt in his pots only if he is properly equipped for that accomplishment.

There are yet other human acts however which by their very nature are never accomplished through instrumentation. There is no Y, for example, such that it would be proper to say that John decided with Y to chase the culprit, and hence no instrument which might be used by John for the making of that decision. This is not to deny that a person might be forced to decide an uncertainty in a particular way by an instrument of persuasion, nor is it to deny that a person might explore various possibilities open to him with a slide rule, an atlas, or another device to aid his memory or calculating powers. It is to deny merely that there is any instrument which can be employed in the act of decision itself. Thus it is also with the acts of vowing, resolving, and demurring, each of which involves either the establishment or the withholding of intention. Finally, the act of intention itself is accomplished, if at all, without use by the intending agent of any other object, agent, or faculty. Thus although we often say things like 'John intended to catch the culprit' and of course say things like 'John intended to catch the culprit with his cane,' we never have occasion to say anything of the form 'X intended *with* Y to do A' which does not fall under one of the other restrictions of (5) above.

It is time now to turn directly to the question whether there are any mechanical acts in which the machine as agent might be said to use an instrument in the accomplishment of the act.

7. It is a feature of artifacts generally that particular goals can be accomplished with them and hence that they are capable of serving as instruments. For present purposes all machines will be considered artifacts. It follows that all machines are capable of being used as instruments.

Now if machines were capable of acting *only* as instruments, the question whether machines themselves can use instruments would be quickly settled by the conditions (1) and (2) above. Given that Y is an instrument in the accomplishment of A only if it is not appropriate to say that Y did-A (condition [2]), then if Y acts only as an instrument, there are no acts which can appropriately be attributed to Y itself. It would follow that there is no act A of which it would be appropriate to say Y did-A with Z and hence (condition [1]) that it is never correct to speak of Y as using an instrument.

This quick solution is not available however, for it is typical of machines that they are capable of acts in which they do not serve as instruments of other agents. The distinction between machines and other artifacts, including "mere tools," coincides generally with the distinction between artifacts which can and those which cannot properly be considered agents in their own right. Machines, that is to say, *do* things which cannot properly be said to be done *with* them by another agent. An engine, for example, might revolve at 4,000 RPM; and, thus functioning, it might be used by a pilot to lift an aircraft off the runway. In this case the revolving is something done by the engine or the shaft, but in no sense by the pilot. And although a person might use a computer to perform a series of arithmetical operations, it is the computer and not the user which adds so and so many digits a microsecond with such and such a probability of error. "Mere tools," on the other hand, generally do only what is done with them. The hammer strikes hard, but only when someone strikes hard with it; and Excalibur cuts deep, but only in the hands of its appointed user.[2]

Among other things done by machines but not done with them are (in the case of engines) to develop horsepower and impart momentum, (computers) to follow instructions and halt at errors, and (computer-based systems) to print out alphanumeric characters and simulate the walking behavior of a human being. Now although these things are done by machines and in each case are accomplished with certain mechanical components, it is not appropriate in each case to describe the doing in the format 'X did-A with Y.' We would not say, for example, that the computer follows instructions *with* its card reader or its core memory, although both components may be involved in its instruction-governed operation. Nor would we say that a computer-based system prints out *with* a line printer, even though a printer of this sort is involved in the system's alphanumeric output.[3] In the former case it is inappropriate to attempt to isolate only one or a few of the computer's components with which to the exclusion of others it might be said to follow instructions. And in the latter case it is more appropriate to say that the printer prints out the characters than to say that the system prints out the characters with the printer, even though it remains appropriate as well to say that the system as a whole prints out the characters. Thus not all cases in which things are done by machines, albeit with the support of mechanical components, are cases in which things are done by machines as instruments. This follows from the failure of cases such as those above to meet condition (1).

There are other cases of mechanical agency in which condition (1) is met, but not condition (2). A rocket engine, for example, is appropriately said to impart momentum with its thrusters, but it is equally appropriate to say that the thrusters impart the momentum. If a computer was installed in a robot to control its motion, again it might seem natural to say that the resulting system simulates the movements of a human being with its mechanical limbs, but it would seem no less appropriate to say merely that the limbs of the robot simulate the walking behavior of a human being. Since it is equally appropriate in such cases to attribute the activity to the system as a whole or to a particular component or set of components of the system, it is not correct to speak of the system as using these components in the accomplishment of the activity.

Instances of mechanical agency nonetheless can be found which meet all four conditions above for the ascription of instrumentality. Advertising in a popular scientific publication, a research corporation recently had this to say in praise of a space-roving power-supply system with an inscrutable name which was then under development: "SNAP-

50/SPUR will employ a nuclear reactor as a heat source to operate turbines that will drive electrical generators." SNAP-50/SPUR is the power system, and the claim of the advertisement is that the system employs a nuclear reactor for a particular purpose, that of driving the electrical generator which transforms the power produced by the system into its output form. The system drives the generator through a series of intermediate energy conversion stages, primary among which is the nuclear reactor. Thus it is appropriate to say that the system drives the generator *with* the nuclear reactor (and with the turbine as well, which also may be said to drive the generator). The reactor itself, however, does not drive the generator, although it might be said to drive the turbine. Conditions (1) and (2) thus are met. Since things other than driving the generator clearly could be, and probably are, done within the system, condition (3) is met as well. And condition (4) is obviously satisfied, inasmuch as the sense of 'with' in question explicitly is one of employment rather than mere accompaniment. There appears to be no reason then why we should not conceive of SNAP-50/SPUR's employment of the nuclear reactor to drive its generator as a case in which a mechanical agent (the system itself) uses an instrument (the reactor) in the accomplishment of a certain specific activity.

Instances of the same can be found from other technological eras. There is a common ring, for example, to the remark that a certain piston-driven engine was able on some occasion to achieve so many RPM with a particular fuel-injection system or that a standard aircraft configuration could do so many MPH with some particular, but nonstandard, engine. Neither the fuel injector nor the engine could in any way here be credited with the performance in question, and clearly other things could be done within their respective systems by either piece of equipment. Since it would be quite wrong to say either that the fuel injector did so many RPM together with the engine or that the engine did so many MPH together with the aircraft, we have in these cases further illustrations of mechanical agency involving the use of instruments. An example from computer technology might come with the claim that a certain data-processing system can read data in and out of storage at the average rate of so many bits a millisecond with a particular drum-storage unit. The drum itself, of course, does not read data in and out at any rate whatsoever and clearly can be used within the system for the distinct purpose of storage without regard to access rates. Since the system does not read data in and out at a particular rate together with the drum, this is something it can be said to do using the drum as instrument.

It might be objected at this point that each of these examples of the use of instruments by machines has been one in which *part* of the mechanical system is used as an instrument for some purpose or another by the system itself as a *whole,* and

INSTRUMENTATION AND MECHANICAL AGENCY 253

that such cases are quite different from the earlier examples of human agency in which the instruments in question always were distinct from the agent himself. The only convincingly parallel example from the sphere of human agency would be one in which part of the agent is used by the agent itself as an instrument. Let us return to human agency in search of such examples.

8. The following locutions indicate that it is commonplace to speak of *using* certain parts of one's own body: 'He has regained use of his limbs,' 'What did he use to put out the flame? His bare hand,' and 'He used his fingers as a plug to stop up the hole.' The sense of 'use' in these locutions moreover is one indicative of instrumentality. For example, (1) we would say 'John put out the flame *with* his bare hand,' (2) it would not seem appropriate to attribute the act to the hand by saying 'John's hand put out the flame,' (3) there are other things John could do with his hand, and (4) we would not say 'John put out the flame together with his hand.' For another example we would say that John stopped the hole with his finger, that it was not his finger but John to whom the act should be attributed, that there are other things John could do with his finger, and that this is not something John did together with his finger. Thus when we say that John used his hand to put out the flame or that he used his finger to stop up the hole, there is nothing against our thinking of the hand or the finger as an instrument with which John accom-

plished the act in question. With respect to the attribution of instrumentality 'He put out the fire with his hand' seems entirely on a par with 'He put out the fire with a wet blanket.' The fact that the hand but not the blanket is part of the agent is not to the point.

Consider as another example the question 'What did he use to break in the door?', with possible answers 'an axe,' 'a large rock,' 'his foot,' and 'his shoulder.' Any one answer is as intelligible as any other, and there is no reason to think (apart from particular circumstances) that only in giving one of the first two answers, but not one of the remainder, would the respondent be naming an instrument involved in the act. Similarly it seems correct to say that among the various instruments one might use to strike a chisel are one's hammer and one's fist, and to say either 'a spoon' or 'her finger' might be entirely appropriate in answer to the question 'What did she use to stir the pudding?'

Now one reason a person might be inclined to deny that an agent could use one of his own limbs as an instrument is that this might seem to lead to an absurd proliferation of instrumentality. Even when using a hammer, one might be said to hammer with one's hand (simply because that is how you hammer); and if we think of a person as using his hand to hold his hammer, why should we not also say that he uses his arm to move his hand, his efferent nerves to control his arm, and so forth? But nothing we have said should encourage such extravagance. Our criteria, on the contrary, would seem to rule out saying even that the hand is an instrument for holding the hammer, and surely to rule out this way of speaking about other parts of the body involved in the act of hammering. We may indeed admit that John could use his hand instead of his trowel to fill his pots. But when the instrument John uses for this purpose is instead his trowel, what John does with his hand is to hold the instrument. And in the act of holding the trowel John would be ruled out from using his hand as another instrument by criterion (2); whereas it would be appropriate to say that John holds his trowel with his hand, it would be equally appropriate to say merely that his hand holds the trowel when John is potting. Moreover we surely would not speak of the shoulder or the nerves as instruments in any of the things John does while potting, since it would be improper in the first place to say that John moved his hand *with* his arm or that he controls his arm *with* his efferent nerves. Although there are things that John might do with his arm, like waving, he neither moves his hand with his arm nor moves his fingers with his knuckles. And it is equally senseless to speak of John doing anything at all with his nerves. What John's nerves do, John does not. Although John might start in surprise, he does not use his nerves to do this; and although his nerves might discharge with unusual frequency in the process, to discharge in this fashion is not among John's accomplishments.

Thus there are parts of John's body which might be used according to our criteria as instruments in one or another of the things John does, and other parts of his body to which we would not attribute instrumentality in any of John's acts. The case of John's body in these respects is instructively parallel to the machine's use of some, but not all, of its components as instruments in the accomplishment of various mechanical acts.

9. It is interesting to note that the criteria of instrumentality do not rule out the conception of John's entire body in some circumstances being used as an instrument by John himself. This suggests one further respect in which human agency might seem to differ from the agency of machines, for it may seem wholly improper at first to think of a machine using its entire self as an instrument.

Circumstances in which John might be considered to use his entire body as an instrument are not common, but examples can be given.[4] If John in an act of heroism was to protect a maiden by blocking a narrow passageway against her pursuers, we might say (1) that John blocked the passageway with his body. In this case it might be correct to say John used his body as an instrument to block the passageway, since (2) we would not say merely that John's *body* blocked the passageway (unless he was dead or unconscious, John did it and not his body), (3) there are other things John could do with his body (protect others from an exploding grenade), and (4) we would not say John blocked the passageway *together* with his body.

This manner of thinking however relies upon a distinction between agent and physical component which, although culturally established for human agency, is not clearly present with regard to mechanical systems or other artifacts. There is no more sense apparent in the remark that an engine used its entire mechanical constituency to overheat than there is in the remark that John's body used John's body to fall over in a dead faint. And while indeed the entire aircraft accelerates through the synchronized operation of all its parts, there is no sense to the suggestion that the aircraft used all its parts, either in conjunction or separately, as an instrument or as instruments of acceleration. Similarly, while the orbital path, or galactic trajectory, of SNAP-50/SPUR depends directly upon the inertial activity of each of its components, the system does not move as it does through the instrumentation of the totality of its parts. The reason in each case here is that there seems to be no conceptual distinction available with reference to which we can distinguish a given mechanical system as agent from the same system in its entirety as contributing to, but not responsible for, the act.

But this conclusion is too tenuous to be of more than temporary interest. Not only are the circumstances in which it would be proper to speak of humans using their entire bodies as instruments rare and difficult to specify but also the very fact that a recognizable difference exists between the "hardware" and the "software" components of a computer-based system suggests a distinction with regard to mechanical agency entirely parallel to that between the human agent and his body. Just as we ordinarily tend to think (unmoved by philosophic problematics involved in the thought) that the person as agent is more than the human body itself, so it is entirely appropriate to think (without resulting philosophic problematics) that the computer-based system is more than the totality of the various pieces of mechanical equipment involved therein. The computer-based guidance system used in orbital space craft, for instance, comprises not only the computer "hardware" on board and on ground but also the inventory of programs available to the computers and the systematized procedures for using various parts of the "hardware" under various expected and unexpected circumstances of over-all system operation. The latter are part of the "software" of the system and as such correspond to those aspects of the human person which we do not conceive as being localized specifically in space and time. But they are part of the system nonetheless. And when we think of the system overall as performing certain functions, it is the integrated combination of "hard" and "software" that we conceive as the agent, not merely the "hardware" components of the system alone.

Thus there is no apparent reason why we should not on occasion speak of a computer-based system which performs in a certain way through the instrumentality of the particular "hardware" as a whole which happens to be associated with it. It might plausibly be said in quite conceivable circumstances, for example, that such and such a computer-based control system resisted impairment by excessively low temperatures with equipment specially constructed in view of this problem. We would not say merely that the *equipment* resisted impairment, since part of the credit is due to the way the system was programmed to react under certain temperature conditions. Conditions (1) and (2) of instrumentation thus are satisfied. Since there obviously are no problems with the two conditions remaining, this appears to be a legitimate illustration of a mechanical act in which the entire physical constituency of the agent serves as an instrument. Thus once again what appeared at first to be a basic difference between human and mechanical agency turns out to be no difference at all.

10. There are problems of mechanical agency and instrumentation which have not been treated in this paper. Among the more interesting and timely at this moment of technological development is whether machines, like people, are capable of using (other) people as instruments. And even if machines and people turn out in the final analysis to be equivalent in their use of instruments, it remains compatible with everything said here that there are other distinctions between human and mechanical agency which will never be smoothed

away. What has been shown is simply that human and mechanical agents cannot be distinguished in any obvious way with reference merely to their respective use of instruments. That this is true however is sufficiently counterintuitive to make it worth the showing.

NOTES

1. The case is more complicated when both X and Y are capable of controlling the behavior of Y in the performance of A. Thus if person X used person Y in the commission of a felony, the deed might be charged in a court of law to both parties. The present discussion of instrumentality deals only with instruments not capable of self-control.

2. The most notable exception lies in the fact that any object might act as it were by accident. The hammer which just happens to be placed upon a piece of paper keeps the paper from blowing in the wind, something attributable to the hammer itself and not normally to the person who happened to lay the hammer in that position. Barring such happenstance, the above-mentioned distinction between machines and other artifacts seems to hold without exception.

3. The term 'computer' here applies only to the equipment for which there is no extra charge in renting or purchasing the machine from the manufacturer. A computer-based system includes "hardware" such as the central computer and various peripheral and inter-

face equipment (for example, cathode-ray tubes and teletype units) and "software" such as standard operational and special purpose programs.

4. It seems incorrect to agree with Hampshire's remark that whereas his arms and legs may be "thought of as instruments which I, distinguished from these instruments, suddenly find that I cannot use," there is no "equivalent sense in which I can be said to use my body, taken as a whole, in bringing about a certain effect or in performing a certain action. . . ." One may agree however that "there is scarcely a conceivable opposition between using my body, taken as a whole, and using something else, my mind." See Stuart Hampshire, *Thought and Action* (London: Chatto and Windus, 1959), p. 80.

Selected Bibliography*

1. Abramson, N. *Information Theory and Coding.* New York: McGraw-Hill, 1963.
2. Allport, F. H. *Theories of Perception and the Concept of Structure.* New York: Holt, Rinehart and Winston, 1959.
3. Arbib, M. *Brains, Machines and Mathematics.* New York: McGraw-Hill, 1964.
4. Ashby, W. *Design for a Brain.* London: Chapman & Hall, 1952.
5. Attnaeve, F. "Symmetry, Information and Memory for Patterns." *American Journal of Psychology,* 68 (1955).

---

* A more comprehensive bibliography has been published in *The Modeling of Mind* by the present editors. See also the bibliography in H. Dreyfus, *Alchemy and Artificial Intelligence,* Rand Corporation paper No. P-3244, December 1965.

6. Attnaeve, F. "Some Informational Aspects of Visual Perception." *Psychological Review,* 61, 3 (1954), 183–193.
7. Austin, J. *Philosophical Papers,* J. O. Urmson and G. J. Warnock, eds. Oxford, at Clarendon Press, 1961.
8. Austin, J. *How to Do Things with Words,* J. O. Urmson, ed. Cambridge, Mass.: Harvard University Press, 1962.
9. Ayer, A. J. "Phenomenology and Linguistic Analysis." *Proceedings of the Aristotelian Society,* supplementary vol. 33 (1959).
10. Baier, K. *The Moral Point of View,* abridged ed. New York: Random House, 1965.
11. Bar-Hillel, Y. "An Examination of Information Theory." *Philosophy of Science,* 22 (1955).
12. Bellman, R. "Dynamic Programming, Intelligent Machines, and Self-Organizing Systems." *1962 Polytechnic Institute of Brooklyn Symposium on Mathematical Theory of Automata.* New York: Polytechnic Institute of Brooklyn Press and Interscience.
13. Berlyne, D. E. "Curiosity and Exploration." *Science,* 153 (July 1, 1966).
14. Berlyne, D. E. *Structure and Direction in Thinking.* New York: John Wiley and Sons, 1965.
15. Bexton, W., Heron, W., and Scott, T. "Effects of Decreased Variation in the Sensory Environment." *Canadian Journal of Psychology,* 8 (1954), 70–76.
16. Brillouin, L. *Science and Information Theory.* New York: Academic Press, 1956.
17. Bush, R., and Mosteller, F. *Stochastic Models for Learning.* New York: John Wiley and Sons, 1955.

18. Carnap, R. "The Two Concepts of Probability." *Philosophy and Phenomenological Research,* vol. 5 (1944–1945), 513–532. Reprinted in *Readings in the Philosophy of Science,* H. Feigl and M. Brodbeck, eds. New York: Appleton-Century-Crofts, Inc., 1953.
19. Carroll, L. "What the Tortoise Said to Achilles." *Mind,* n.s. 4, 14 (1895), 278–280.
20. Cooper, D. "The Automated Laboratory." *International Science and Technology,* 36 (December 1964), 20–29.
21. Crosson, F. J. "Formal Logic and Formal Ontology in Husserl's Phenomenology." *Notre Dame Journal of Formal Logic,* 3, 4 (October 1962), 259–269.
22. Culbertson, J. *The Minds of Robots.* Urbana: University of Illinois Press, 1963.
23. Danto, E. "On Consciousness in Machines." *Dimensions of Mind,* S. Hook, ed. New York: Collier Books, 1960.
24. Daveney, T. F. "Choosing." *Mind,* 73 (October 1964).
25. Davis, M. *Computability and Unsolvability.* New York: McGraw-Hill, 1958.
26. Dewey, J. *Intelligence in the Modern World.* J. Ratner, ed. New York: Modern Library, 1939.
27. Dreyfus, H. "Alchemy and Artificial Intelligence." *Rand Report,* P-3244 (1965).
28. Eccles, J. *Neurophysiological Basis of Mind.* Oxford: Oxford University Press, 1953.
29. Elsasser, W. *The Physical Foundations of Biology.* New York: Pergamon Press, 1958.
30. Evans, D. D. *The Logic of Self-Involvement.* London: SCM Press, 1963.

31. Evans, J. L. "Choice." *The Philosophical Quarterly*, 5, 21 (1955).
32. Feigl, H. "The 'Mental' and the 'Physical'." *Minnesota Studies in the Philosophy of Science*, vol. 2. Minneapolis: University of Minnesota Press, 1958, 370–497.
33. Feller, W. *An Introduction to Probability Theory and its Applications*. New York: John Wiley and Sons, 1950.
34. Gallagher, K. T. "On Choosing to Choose." *Mind*, 63 (October 1964).
35. Geach, P. *Mental Acts*. London: Routledge and Kegan Paul, 1957.
36. George, F. *Cybernetics and Biology*. Edinburg: Oliver and Boyd, 1965.
37. Gerard, R. "What is Memory." in *Scientific American*, 189, 3 (1953).
38. Glasgow, W. D. "On Choosing," *Analysis*, 17 (1956–1957).
39. Gödel, K. "Über formal unentscheidbare Sätze der Principia Mathematica und verwandter systeme." *Monatshefte für Mathematik und Physik*, 38 (1931), 173–198.
40. Gurwitsch, A. *The Field of Consciousness*. Pittsburgh: Duquesne University Press, 1964.
41. Hampshire, S. *Thought and Action*. London: Chatto and Windus, 1959.
42. Hartley, R. "Transmission of Information." *Bell System Technical Journal*, 7 (1928), 535–563.
43. Hartman, G. *Gestalt Psychology*. New York: The Ronald Press Co., 1935.
44. Hiller, L., and Baker, R. "Computer Cantata: A Study in Compositional Method." *Perspectives of New Music*, 3 (1964), 62–90.

45. Hiller, L., and Isaacson, L. *Experimental Music*. New York: McGraw-Hill, 1959.
46. Hochberg, J., and McAlister, E. "A Quantitative Approach to Figural Goodness," *Journal of Experimental Psychology*, 46, 5 (1953), 361–364.
47. Hume, D. *A Treatise of Human Nature*. Oxford: Clarendon Press, 1960.
48. Hume, D. *Enquiry Concerning the Human Understanding*. Oxford: Clarendon Press, 1961.
49. Husserl, E. *Cartesian Meditations*, D. Cairns, trans. The Hague: Nijhoff, 1960.
50. Husserl, E. *Erfahrung und Urteil*. Hamburg: Classen & Goverts, 1948.
51. Husserl, E. *Ideas*, W. R. B. Gibson, trans. New York: Crowell-Collier, 1962.
52. Husserl, E. *Logische Untersuchungen*, vol. 2. Halle: Niemeyer, 1928.
53. Krech, D., and Crutchfield, R. *Elements of Psychology*. New York: Knopf, 1959.
54. Leeper, R. W. "A Study of a Neglected Portion of the Field of Learning: The Development of Sensory Organization." *Journal of Genetic Psychology*, 46 (1935).
55. Lewis, C. I. "The Modes of Meaning." *Philosophy and Phenomenological Research*, 4 (1944).
56. Licklider, J. "Man-Computer Symbiosis." *IRE Transactions on Human Factors in Electronics*, HFE-1 (March 1960).
57. Lindegren, Nilo. "Cursive Script Recognition." Part 3 of "Machine Recognition of Human Language." *Spectrum* (May 1965), 104–116.
58. Lucas, J. "Minds, Machines and Gödel." *Philosophy* (1961), 112–126. Reprinted in *The Modeling of Mind*, K. Sayre and F. Crosson, eds. Notre

Dame: University of Notre Dame Press, 1963.
59. MacKay, D. M. "Mindlike Behaviour in Artefacts." *British Journal for the Philosophy of Science*, 2 (1951–1952), 105–121. Reprinted in *The Modeling of Mind*, K. Sayre and F. Crosson, eds. Notre Dame: University of Notre Dame Press, 1963.
60. MacKay, D. M. "The Informational Analysis of Questions and Commands." *Information Theory: 4th London Symposium*, C. Cherry, ed. London: Butterworth and Co., Inc., 1961.
61. Marhenke, P. "The Criterion of Significance." *Semantics and the Philosophy of Language*, L. Linsky, ed. Urbana: University of Illinois Press, 1952.
62. Merleau-Ponty, M. *Phenomenology of Perception*, C. Smith, trans. New York: Humanities Press, 1962.
63. Meyer, L. "Meaning in Music and Information Theory." *Journal of Aesthetics and Art Criticism*, 15, 4 (1957), 412–424.
64. Meyers, C. M. "The Determinate and Determinable Modes of Appearing." *Mind*, 67 (1958), 32–49.
65. Miller, G. "Human Memory and Storage of Information." *IRE Transactions of Information Theory*, 1 T-2, 3 (1956).
66. Norwell-Smith, P. H. "Choosing, Deciding and Doing." *Analysis*, 18 (1957–1958).
67. Peirce, C. *Collected Papers*. Cambridge: Harvard University Press, 1931.
68. Quastler, H. *Information Theory in Psychology*. Glencoe, Illinois: Free Press, 1955.
69. Ralls, A. "Game of Life." *Philosophical Quarterly*, 16 (1966), 23–34.

70. Ryle, G. *Concept of Mind*. New York: Barnes and Noble, 1949.
71. Sayre, K. M. *Recognition: A Study in the Philosophy of Artificial Intelligence*. Notre Dame: University of Notre Dame Press, 1965.
72. Sayre, K., and Crosson, F., eds. *The Modeling of Mind*. Notre Dame: University of Notre Dame Press, 1963.
73. Scriven, M. "The Compleat Robot: A Prolegomena to Androidology." *Dimensions of Mind*, S. Hook, ed. New York: Collier Books, 1960, 113–133.
74. Scriven, M. "The Mechanical Concept of Mind." Reprinted in *The Modeling of Mind*, K. Sayre and F. Crosson, eds. Notre Dame: University of Notre Dame Press, 1963.
75. Searle, J. "How to Derive 'Ought' from 'Is.'" *Philosophical Review*, 73 (1964), 55; relying on J. Rawls, "Two Concepts of Rules." *Philosophical Review*, 64 (1955), 3–32.
76. Selfridge, O. "Pandemonium: A Paradigm for Learning." *Mechanisation of Thought Processes*, vol. 1, Blake and Uttley, eds. London: Her Majesty's Stationery Office, 1959, 513–526.
77. Sender, J. W. "Human Performance." *International Science and Technology*, 55 (July 1966), 58–68.
78. Shannon, C. "A Mathematical Theory of Communication." *Bell System Technical Journal*, 27 (1948), 379–423, 623–656.
79. Shannon, C. "Prediction and Entropy of Printed English." *Bell System Technical Journal*, 30 (1951), 50–64.
80. Shannon, C. and Weaver, W. *The Mathematical*

Theory of Communication. Urbana, Illinois: University of Illinois Press, 1949.
81. Sluckin, W. *Minds and Machines.* London: Penguin, 1960.
82. Smart, J. *Philosophy and Scientific Realism.* London: Routledge & Kegan Paul, 1963.
83. Smith, N. K. *The Philosophy of David Hume.* London: Macmillan, 1964.
84. Szilard, L. "Über die Entropieverminderung in einem thermodynamischen System bei Eingriffen intelligenter Wesen." *Zeitschrift für Physik,* 53 (1929).
85. Tillman, F., and Russel, B. "Language, Information, and Entropy." *Logigue et Analyse,* 30 (1965).
86. Veatch, H. *Rational Man: A Modern Interpretation of Aristotelian Ethics.* Bloomington: Indiana University Press, 1962.
87. Walter, W. *The Living Brain.* New York: Norton & Co., 1953.
88. Wang, H. "Towards Mechanical Mathematics." *IBM Journal of Research and Development,* 4 (1960), 2–22. Reprinted in *The Modeling of Mind,* K. Sayre and F. Crosson, eds. Notre Dame: University of Notre Dame Press, 1963.
89. Wiener, N. *Cybernetics.* New York: The Technology Press and John Wiley and Sons, Inc., 1948. 2nd ed., Cambridge: M.I.T. Press.
90. Wiener, N. *God and Golem, Inc.* Cambridge: M.I.T. Press, 1964.
91. Wiener, N. *The Human Use of Human Beings: Cybernetics and Society.* Boston: Houghton Mifflin Co., 1950. 2nd ed. rev., Garden City: New York, Doubleday & Co., Inc., 1954.

92. Weizanbaum, J. "ELIZA—A Computer Program for the Study of Natural Language Communication Between Man and Machine." *Communications of the ACM*, 9, 1 (January 1966), 36–43.
93. Wittgenstein, L. *Philosophical Investigations.* New York: MacMillan, 1953.
94. Wittgenstein, L. *Remarks on the Foundation of Mathematics.* New York: MacMillan, 1956.
95. Wooldridge, D. *The Machinery of the Brain.* New York: McGraw-Hill, 1963.
96. Zubeck, J. "Behavioral and EEG Changes after 14 Days of Perceptual Deprivation." *Psychonomic Science*, 1 (1964).

Q
315
P5

JUL 9 - 1971